P9-EKD-884

CALGARY PUBLIC LIBRARY

MAR     2011

# Pattern + Palette⁴

## SOURCEBOOK

ROCKPORT

© 2010 by Rockport Publishers, Inc.

All rights reserved. No part of this book may be reproduced in any form without written permission of the copyright owners. All images in this book have been reproduced with the knowledge and prior consent of the artists concerned, and no responsibility is accepted by producer, publisher, or printer for any infringement of copyright or otherwise, arising from the contents of this publication. Every effort has been made to ensure that credits accurately comply with information supplied. We apologize for any inaccuracies that may have occurred and will resolve inaccurate or missing information in a subsequent reprinting of the book.

First published in the United States of America by
Rockport Publishers, a member of
Quayside Publishing Group
100 Cummings Center
Suite 406-L
Beverly, Massachusetts 01915-6101
Telephone: (978) 282-9590
Fax: (978) 283-2742
www.rockpub.com


ISBN-13: 978-1-59253-604-7
ISBN-10: 1-59253-604-2

**Library of Congress Control Number: 2010931295**


10  9  8  7  6  5  4  3  2  1


Series Design: Anvil Graphic Design, Inc.
Cover Design: Harvey Rayner
Layout and Production: Kathie Alexander


Printed in Singapore

# Pattern + Palette⁴
## SOURCEBOOK

A Comprehensive Guide to
Choosing the Perfect Color
and Pattern in Design

Kathie Alexander and
Harvey Rayner

BEVERLY MASSACHUSETTS

ROCKPORT PUBLISHERS

**Includes**
Copyright-Free
Vector Files for
All Patterns

# Contents

*Pattern and Palette Sourcebook 4* is a comprehensive guide to sophisticated patterns and color combinations. Use this book and the accompanying CD-ROM as an inspiring tool to provide you with unconventional insights into the nature and application of color combinations and pattern designs to use in your own projects. Because color preferences are of personal choice and very subjective, enjoy exploring the Technicolor pages of this guide with curiosity and an open mind.

The philosophy of this manual is based on interpretation; in this case, the interpretation of the designers. Harvey Rayner has created one-hundred-fifty pattern designs to which designer, Kathie Alexander, created color themes to produce nine-hundred-fifty unique patterns and color combinations. The themes include: Dark Glamour, Life Luxuries, Color Moods, Galaxy, Reinventing, and Globe-trotter. With these artfully designed palettes, she has created a framework for trends in color and patterns.

Each page showcases five examples of patterns that were developed using two or more of the color samples at the top of the page. By studying and experimenting with these patterns, you can see how any two or more colors work together to create astonishingly different effects. The same coordinated set of colors can say vastly different things, depending on how they are assembled and applied. All the patterns and color combinations are included on the enclosed disc and are copyright free for you to alter the colors according to your needs and use in your own projects.

# Dark Glamour

Timeless elegance is what these palettes reflect. Inspired by rich velvets, metallic sheens, and romantic hues, Gothic and art deco come together to create colors that are alluring and excite the senses.

By combining blacks and browns the following colors evoke passion, power, reliability, and stability.

| | |
|---|---|
| C 82 | 28 |
| M 0 | 0 |
| Y 28 | 29 |
| K 52 | 48 |
| 20 | 0 |
| 20 | 2 |
| 20 | 8 |
| 100 | 10 |
| 45 | 6 |
| 100 | 6 |
| 0 | 0 |
| 55 | 5 |

001

002

003

004

005

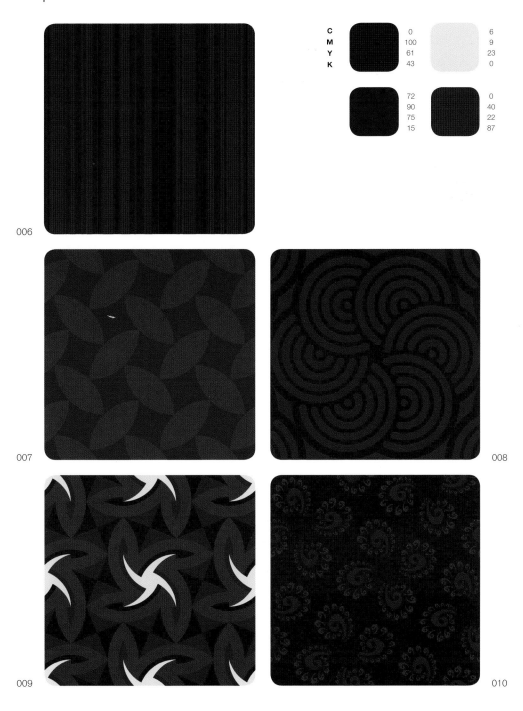

006

| | | | |
|---|---|---|---|
| **C** | 0 | 6 |
| **M** | 100 | 9 |
| **Y** | 61 | 23 |
| **K** | 43 | 0 |

| | |
|---|---|
| 72 | 0 |
| 90 | 40 |
| 75 | 22 |
| 15 | 87 |

007

008

009

010

| C | 0 | | 28 |
|---|---|---|---|
| M | 2 | | 0 |
| Y | 8 | | 29 |
| K | 10 | | 48 |

| | 82 | | 0 |
|---|---|---|---|
| | 0 | | 8 |
| | 28 | | 14 |
| | 52 | | 38 |

011

012

013

014

015

| | |
|---|---|
| **C** | 6 |
| **M** | 6 |
| **Y** | 0 |
| **K** | 5 |

| | |
|---|---|
| 13 |
| 0 |
| 100 |
| 46 |

| | |
|---|---|
| 0 |
| 8 |
| 14 |
| 38 |

016

017

018

019

020

| | C | | |
| --- | --- | --- | --- |
| C | 6 | | 0 |
| M | 9 | | 8 |
| Y | 23 | | 14 |
| K | 0 | | 38 |
| | 0 | | 0 |
| | 40 | | 15 |
| | 22 | | 100 |
| | 87 | | 28 |

021

022

023

024

025

026

| | | | | |
|---|---|---|---|---|
| C | 46 | | 20 | |
| M | 45 | | 20 | |
| Y | 49 | | 20 | |
| K | 0 | | 100 | |

| | |
|---|---|
| 45 | |
| 100 | |
| 0 | |
| 55 | |

027

028

029

030

| | | | | |
|---|---|---|---|---|
| **C** | 6 | | 6 | |
| **M** | 9 | | 6 | |
| **Y** | 23 | | 0 | |
| **K** | 0 | | 5 | |
| | 13 | | 0 | |
| | 0 | | 73 | |
| | 100 | | 100 | |
| | 46 | | 80 | |

031

032

033

034

035

036

037

038

039

040

C 0 6
M 58 6
Y 100 0
K 33 5

0 6
15 9
100 23
28 0

| C | 20 | | 6 |
| M | 20 | | 6 |
| Y | 20 | | 0 |
| K | 100 | | 5 |

| | 0 | | 0 |
| | 59 | | 2 |
| | 48 | | 0 |
| | 48 | | 60 |

041

042

043

044

045

| | C | 82 | | 0 |
| | M | 0 | | 40 |
| | Y | 28 | | 22 |
| | K | 52 | | 87 |

| | 6 | | 0 |
| | 9 | | 59 |
| | 23 | | 48 |
| | 0 | | 48 |

046

047

048

049

050

| | C | M | Y | K |
|---|---|---|---|---|
| | 0 | 0 | 0 | 29 |
| | 82 | 0 | 28 | 52 |
| | 0 | 3 | 55 | 87 |

051

052

053

054

055

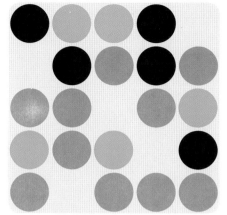

056

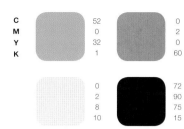

| | | |
|---|---|---|
| **C** | | 52 |
| **M** | | 0 |
| **Y** | | 32 |
| **K** | | 1 |

| | |
|---|---|
| | 0 |
| | 2 |
| | 0 |
| | 60 |

| | |
|---|---|
| | 0 |
| | 2 |
| | 8 |
| | 10 |

| | |
|---|---|
| | 72 |
| | 90 |
| | 75 |
| | 15 |

057

058

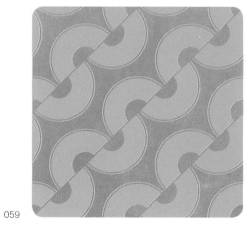

059

060

| C | 0 | | 46 |
| M | 15 | | 45 |
| Y | 100 | | 49 |
| K | 28 | | 0 |

| | 0 | | 6 |
| | 2 | | 9 |
| | 0 | | 23 |
| | 60 | | 0 |

061

062

063

064

065

C M Y K

82 0 28 52

52 0 32 1

0 2 8 10

066

067

068

069

070

| | | |
|---|---|---|
| C | 0 | 0 |
| M | 8 | 40 |
| Y | 14 | 22 |
| K | 38 | 87 |
| | 0 | 7 |
| | 100 | 9 |
| | 36 | 10 |
| | 37 | 0 |

071

072

073

074

075

| | | | | |
|---|---|---|---|---|
| C | 6 | | 30 | |
| M | 6 | | 4 | |
| Y | 0 | | 0 | |
| K | 5 | | 31 | |
| | 0 | | 0 | |
| | 8 | | 2 | |
| | 14 | | 0 | |
| | 38 | | 60 | |
| | | 0 | | |
| | | 40 | | |
| | | 22 | | |
| | | 87 | | |

076

077

078

079

080

| C | 0 | 0 |
| M | 58 | 8 |
| Y | 100 | 14 |
| K | 33 | 38 |

| 0 | 0 |
| 17 | 40 |
| 50 | 22 |
| 65 | 87 |

| 0 |
| 2 |
| 0 |
| 60 |

081

082

083

084

085

| C | | 72 | | 0 |
|---|---|----|---|---|
| M | | 90 | | 2 |
| Y | | 75 | | 8 |
| K | | 15 | | 10 |

| | 45 | | 0 |
|---|----|---|---|
| | 100 | | 8 |
| | 0 | | 14 |
| | 55 | | 38 |

087

088

089

090

| C | 20 | | 0 |
|---|---|---|---|
| M | 20 | | 59 |
| Y | 20 | | 48 |
| K | 100 | | 48 |

| | 0 | | 0 |
|---|---|---|---|
| | 17 | | 58 |
| | 50 | | 100 |
| | 65 | | 33 |

091

092

093

094

095

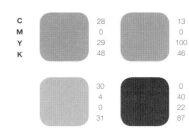

| C | 28 | 13 |
|---|----|----|
| M | 0 | 0 |
| Y | 29 | 100 |
| K | 48 | 46 |

| | 30 | 0 |
|---|----|----|
| | 4 | 40 |
| | 0 | 22 |
| | 31 | 87 |

096

097

098

099

100

| | | |
|---|---|---|
| C | 45 | 46 |
| M | 100 | 45 |
| Y | 0 | 49 |
| K | 55 | 0 |
| | 52 | 6 |
| | 0 | 6 |
| | 32 | 0 |
| | 1 | 5 |

101

102

103

104

105

| | | | |
|---|---|---|---|
| C | 30 | | 0 |
| M | 4 | | 40 |
| Y | 0 | | 22 |
| K | 31 | | 87 |

| | | |
|---|---|---|
| 0 | | 7 |
| 8 | | 9 |
| 14 | | 10 |
| 38 | | 0 |

106

107

108

109

110

| | | | |
|---|---|---|---|
| **C** | 13 | | 0 |
| **M** | 0 | | 2 |
| **Y** | 100 | | 0 |
| **K** | 46 | | 60 |

| | | | |
|---|---|---|---|
| | 20 | | 0 |
| | 20 | | 8 |
| | 20 | | 14 |
| | 100 | | 38 |

111

112

113

114

115

116

117

118

119

120

| | C | M | Y | K |
|---|---|---|---|---|
| | 0 | 82 | 52 | 0 |
| | 2 | 0 | 0 | 58 |
| | 8 | 28 | 32 | 100 |
| | 10 | 52 | 1 | 33 |

121

122

123

124

125

| C | 28 | | 20 |
| M | 0 | | 20 |
| Y | 29 | | 20 |
| K | 48 | | 100 |

| | 0 | | 0 |
| | 8 | | 59 |
| | 14 | | 48 |
| | 38 | | 48 |

126

127

128

129

130

| C | | |
|---|---|---|
| M | 0 | 0 |
| Y | 8 | 58 |
| K | 14 | 100 |
| | 38 | 33 |

| 13 | 0 |
|---|---|
| 0 | 17 |
| 100 | 50 |
| 46 | 65 |

| 0 |
|---|
| 2 |
| 0 |
| 60 |

131

132

133

134

135

| | |
|---|---|
| **C** 72 | 0 |
| **M** 90 | 100 |
| **Y** 75 | 36 |
| **K** 15 | 37 |

| |
|---|
| 0 |
| 2 |
| 0 |
| 60 |

136

137

138

139

140

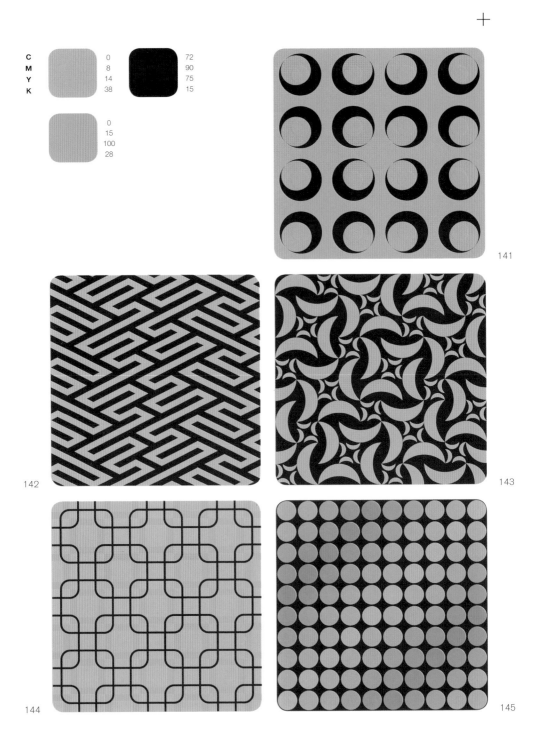

| | | |
|---|---|---|
| C | | 0 |
| M | | 8 |
| Y | | 14 |
| K | | 38 |

| | |
|---|---|
| 72 |
| 90 |
| 75 |
| 15 |

| | |
|---|---|
| 0 |
| 15 |
| 100 |
| 28 |

141

142

143

144

145

146

147

148

149

150

| C | M | Y | K | | C | M | Y | K |
|---|---|---|---|---|---|---|---|---|
| 6 | 9 | 23 | 0 | | 13 | 0 | 100 | 46 |
| 0 | 40 | 22 | 87 | | 82 | 0 | 28 | 52 |

156

45
100
0
55

0
8
14
38

6
9
23
0

157

158

159

160

**Dark Glamour** 39

# Life Luxuries

Today's younger eco-minded generation is redefining luxury. A natural color palette is no longer inspired by Mother Nature. The colors in this section are influenced by recycled materials and thrift store finds. The new modern way of life is about ethical indulgence.

People are traveling to rediscover and celebrate their heritage. They surround themselves with color memories from all over the world. Handmade materials, root dyes, and organic cuisine are just a few areas to explore when selecting today's luxurious color palettes.

| | |
|---|---|
| **C** | 50 |
| **M** | 0 |
| **Y** | 25 |
| **K** | 30 |

| | |
|---|---|
| | 10 |
| | 0 |
| | 3 |
| | 16 |

| | |
|---|---|
| | 0 |
| | 0 |
| | 91 |
| | 79 |

| | |
|---|---|
| | 23 |
| | 2 |
| | 0 |
| | 63 |

| | |
|---|---|
| | 0 |
| | 4 |
| | 22 |
| | 32 |

161

162

163

164

165

| | |
|---|---|
| **C** | 50 |
| **M** | 0 |
| **Y** | 25 |
| **K** | 30 |

| |
|---|
| 0 |
| 4 |
| 22 |
| 32 |

| |
|---|
| 10 |
| 0 |
| 3 |
| 16 |

| |
|---|
| 0 |
| 100 |
| 63 |
| 29 |

| |
|---|
| 0 |
| 55 |
| 100 |
| 64 |

| |
|---|
| 50 |
| 58 |
| 100 |
| 45 |

171

172

173

174

175

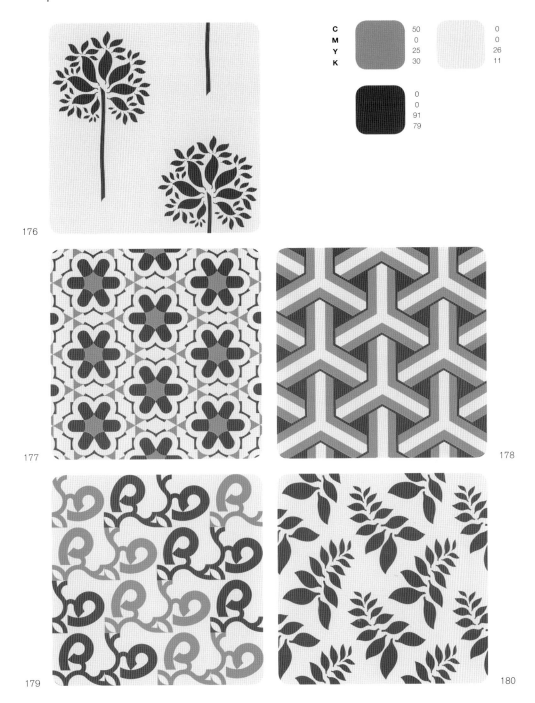

| C | 50 | | 0 |
|---|---|---|---|
| M | 0 | | 0 |
| Y | 25 | | 26 |
| K | 30 | | 11 |

| C | 0 |
|---|---|
| M | 0 |
| Y | 91 |
| K | 79 |

176

177

178

179

180

| C | 23 | | 10 |
|---|----|---|----|
| M | 2 | | 0 |
| Y | 0 | | 3 |
| K | 63 | | 16 |

| | 0 |
|---|---|
| | 4 |
| | 22 |
| | 32 |

181

182

183

184

185

186

| | | 0 | | 19 |
|---|---|---|---|---|
| C | | 0 | | 0 |
| M | | 91 | | 6 |
| Y | | 79 | | 0 |
| K | | | | |
| | 0 | | 0 | |
| | 0 | | 4 | |
| | 20 | | 22 | |
| | 4 | | 32 | |

187

188

189

190

| | | | |
|---|---|---|---|
| **C** | 19 | | 0 |
| **M** | 0 | | 31 |
| **Y** | 6 | | 62 |
| **K** | 0 | | 18 |
| | 0 | | 23 |
| | 55 | | 2 |
| | 100 | | 0 |
| | 64 | | 63 |

191

192

193

194

195

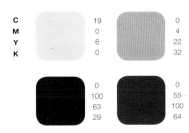

| | | | |
|---|---|---|---|
| **C** | 19 | | 0 |
| **M** | 0 | | 4 |
| **Y** | 6 | | 22 |
| **K** | 0 | | 32 |

| | | | |
|---|---|---|---|
| | 0 | | 0 |
| | 100 | | 55 |
| | 63 | | 100 |
| | 29 | | 64 |

196

197

198

199

200

| | C | M | Y | K |
|---|---|---|---|---|
| | 0 | 0 | | |
| | 5 | 0 | | |
| | 100 | 20 | | |
| | 53 | 4 | | |
| | 55 | 80 | | |
| | 30 | 15 | | |
| | 0 | 0 | | |
| | 0 | 45 | | |
| | 25 | 0 | | |
| | 7 | 55 | | |
| | 0 | 100 | | |
| | 4 | 64 | | |

201

202

203

204

205

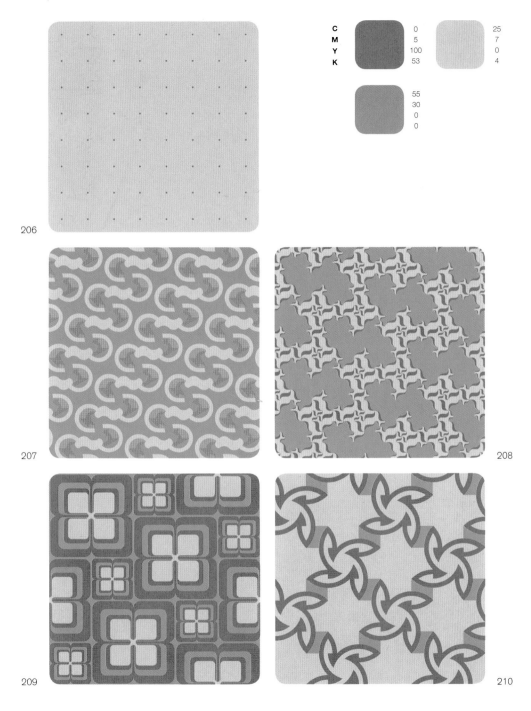

| C | 0 | 25 |
| M | 5 | 7 |
| Y | 100 | 0 |
| K | 53 | 4 |

55
30
0
0

206

207

208

209

210

| C | 0 | | 25 |
|---|---|---|---|
| M | 0 | | 7 |
| Y | 20 | | 0 |
| K | 4 | | 4 |

| | 0 | | 5 |
|---|---|---|---|
| | 55 | | 0 |
| | 100 | | 40 |
| | 64 | | 0 |

| | 23 |
|---|---|
| | 2 |
| | 0 |
| | 63 |

211

212

213

214

215

216

| | | |
|---|---|---|
| **C** | 55 | 23 |
| **M** | 30 | 2 |
| **Y** | 0 | 0 |
| **K** | 0 | 63 |
| | 25 | 0 |
| | 7 | 55 |
| | 0 | 100 |
| | 4 | 64 |

217

218

219

220

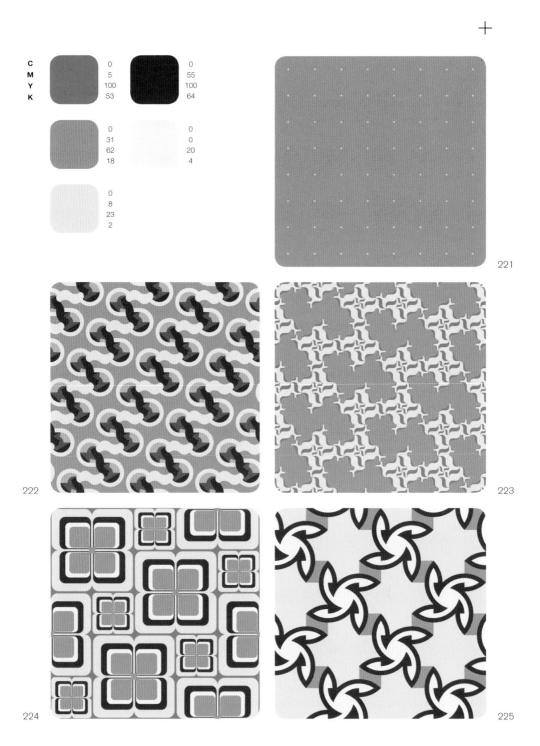

| C | M | Y | K |
|---|---|---|---|
| 0 | 5 | 100 | 53 |
| 0 | 55 | 100 | 64 |
| 0 | 31 | 62 | 18 |
| 0 | 0 | 20 | 4 |
| 0 | 8 | 23 | 2 |

221

222

223

224

225

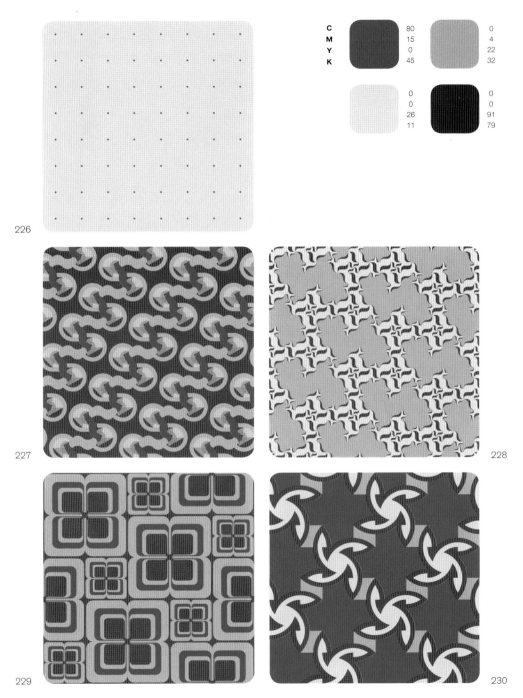

| C | | 80 | | 0 |
| M | | 15 | | 4 |
| Y | | 0 | | 22 |
| K | | 45 | | 32 |

| | 0 | | 0 |
| | 0 | | 0 |
| | 26 | | 91 |
| | 11 | | 79 |

226

227

228

229

230

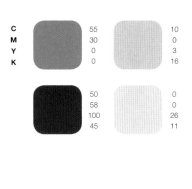

| | C | M | Y | K | | | C | M | Y | K |
|---|---|---|---|---|---|---|---|---|---|---|

C 55
M 30
Y 0
K 0

10
0
3
16

50
58
100
45

0
0
26
11

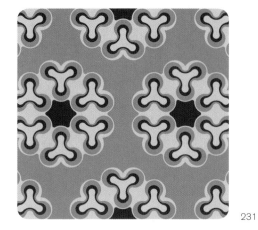

231

232

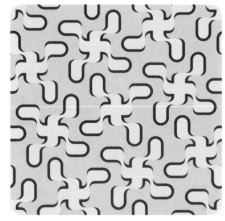

233

234

235

236

237

238

239

240

| C | 23 | | 5 |
|---|----|---|---|
| M | 2 | | 0 |
| Y | 0 | | 40 |
| K | 63 | | 0 |

| 0 | | 0 |
|---|---|---|
| 4 | | 27 |
| 22 | | 100 |
| 32 | | 34 |

| | C | M | Y | K | | C | M | Y | K |
|---|---|---|---|---|---|---|---|---|---|
| | 47 | 0 | 11 | 0 | | 0 | 53 | 100 | 4 |
| | 0 | 52 | 100 | 54 | | 0 | 31 | 62 | 18 |
| | 19 | 0 | 6 | 0 | | 0 | 0 | 20 | 4 |

241

242

243

244

245

C 47 0
M 0 0
Y 11 91
K 0 79

19 5
0 0
6 40
0 0

246

247

248

249

250

| C | | |
|---|---|---|
| M | 0 | 0 |
| Y | 55 | 0 |
| K | 100 | 91 |
| | 64 | 79 |

| | |
|---|---|
| 0 | 0 |
| 31 | 8 |
| 62 | 23 |
| 18 | 2 |

| |
|---|
| 0 |
| 0 |
| 20 |
| 4 |

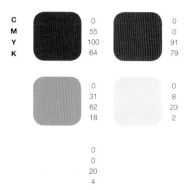

251

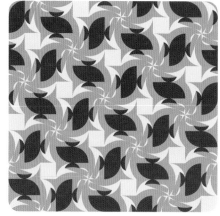

252

253

254

255

256

257

258

259

260

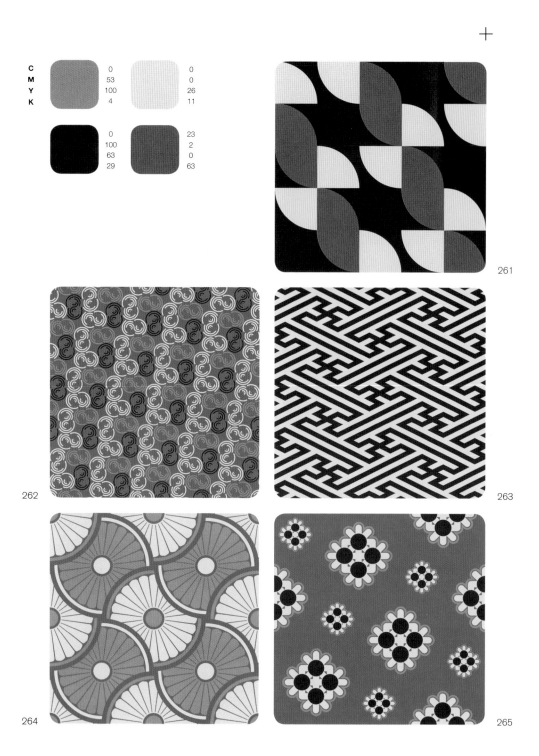

| | | | |
|---|---|---|---|
| C | 0 | 0 | |
| M | 53 | 0 | |
| Y | 100 | 26 | |
| K | 4 | 11 | |
| | 0 | 23 | |
| | 100 | 2 | |
| | 63 | 0 | |
| | 29 | 63 | |

261

262

263

264

265

266

C 0       50
M 27     0
Y 100   25
K 34    30

5     19
0     0
40   6
0     0

267

268

269

270

| C | 47 | | 0 |
|---|----|---|---|
| M | 0 | | 0 |
| Y | 11 | | 26 |
| K | 0 | | 11 |

| | 0 | | 0 |
|---|----|---|---|
| | 31 | | 0 |
| | 62 | | 15 |
| | 18 | | 82 |

271

272

273

274

275

| | | 0 | | 0 |
|---|---|---|---|---|
| C | | 53 | | 4 |
| M | | 100 | | 22 |
| Y | | 4 | | 32 |
| K | | | | |

276

277

278

279

280

| | C | M | Y | K |
|---|---|---|---|---|
| | 32 | 0 | 24 | 10 |
| | 0 | 27 | 100 | 34 |
| | 0 | 47 | 41 | 0 |
| | 0 | 91 | 100 | 60 |
| | 0 | 0 | 15 | 82 |
| | 5 | 40 | 0 | 0 |

281

282

283

284

285

| | | |
|---|---|---|
| **C** | | 0 |
| **M** | | 27 |
| **Y** | | 100 |
| **K** | | 34 |

| | |
|---|---|
| 0 |
| 47 |
| 41 |
| 0 |

| | |
|---|---|
| 0 |
| 0 |
| 15 |
| 82 |

| | |
|---|---|
| 5 |
| 0 |
| 40 |
| 0 |

286

287

288

289

290

**Life Luxuries** 67

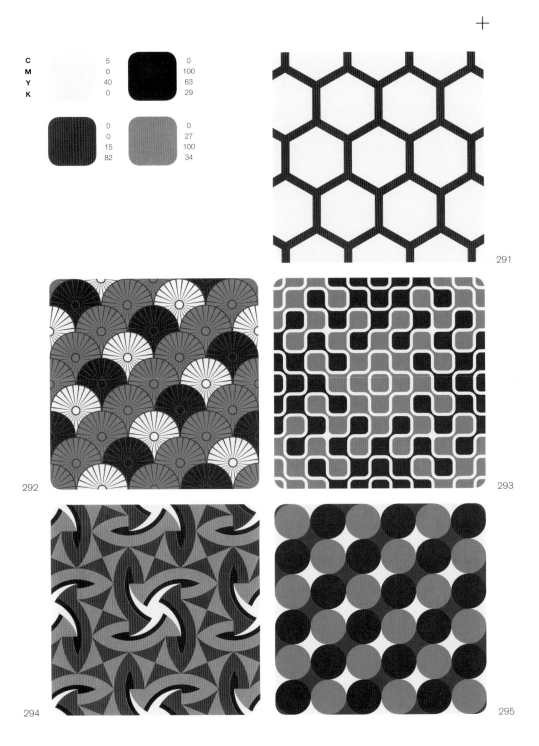

| | | | |
|---|---|---|---|
| **C** | 5 | | 0 |
| **M** | 0 | | 100 |
| **Y** | 40 | | 63 |
| **K** | 0 | | 29 |
| | 0 | | 0 |
| | 0 | | 27 |
| | 15 | | 100 |
| | 82 | | 34 |

291

292

293

294

295

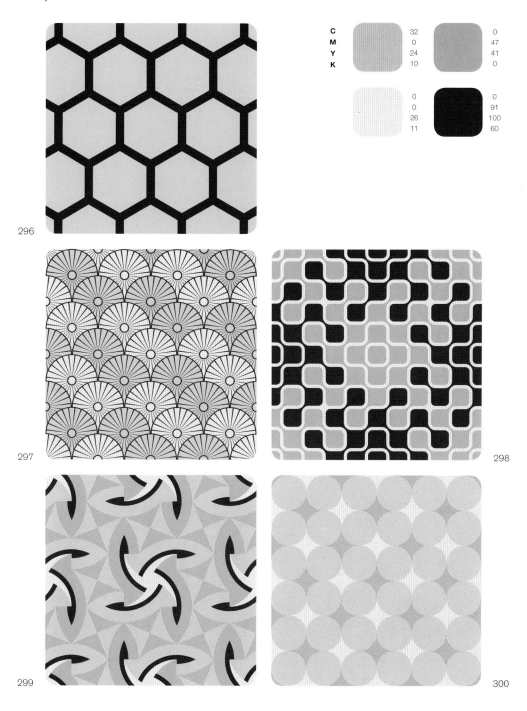

| | | | | |
|---|---|---|---|---|
| **C** | | 32 | | 0 |
| **M** | | 0 | | 47 |
| **Y** | | 24 | | 41 |
| **K** | | 10 | | 0 |
| | | 0 | | 0 |
| | | 0 | | 91 |
| | | 26 | | 100 |
| | | 11 | | 60 |

296

297

298

299

300

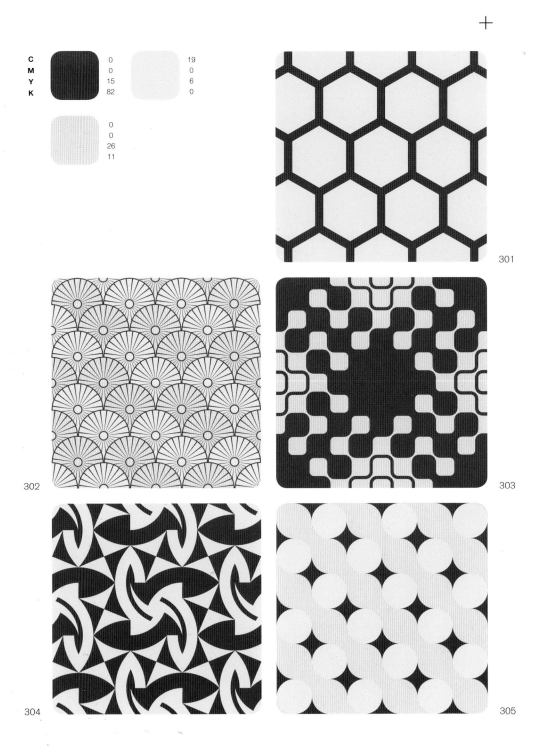

| | C | 0 | | 19 |
|---|---|---|---|---|
| | M | 0 | | 0 |
| | Y | 15 | | 6 |
| | K | 82 | | 0 |

| | 0 |
|---|---|
| | 0 |
| | 26 |
| | 11 |

301

302

303

304

305

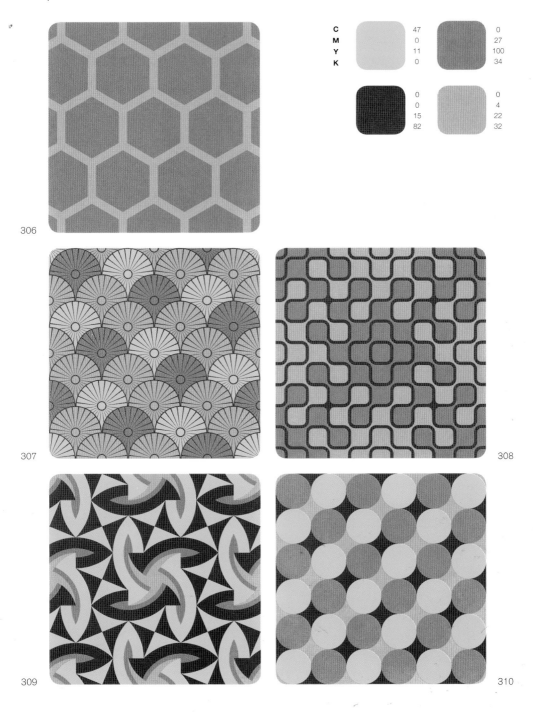

| C | 47 | | 0 |
|---|----|---|---|
| M | 0  | | 27 |
| Y | 11 | | 100 |
| K | 0  | | 34 |

| | 0 | | 0 |
|---|----|---|---|
| | 0  | | 4 |
| | 15 | | 22 |
| | 82 | | 32 |

306

307

308

309

310

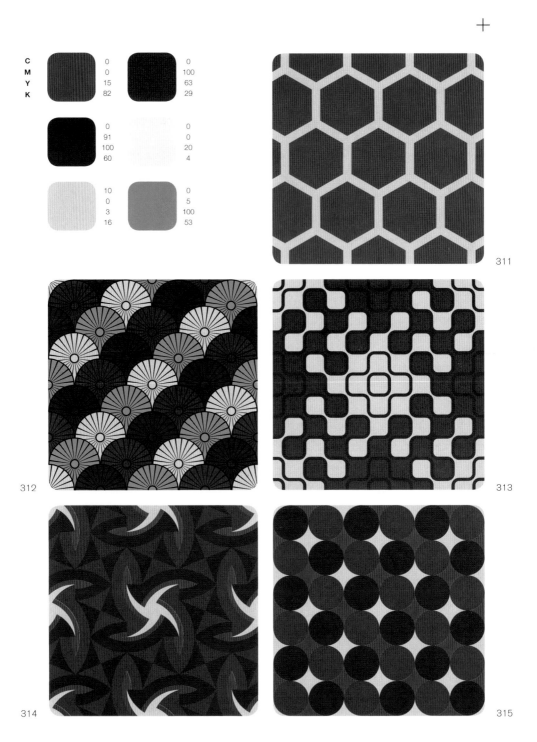

| C | 0 | | 0 |
|---|---|---|---|
| M | 0 | | 100 |
| Y | 15 | | 63 |
| K | 82 | | 29 |

| | 0 | | 0 |
|---|---|---|---|
| | 91 | | 0 |
| | 100 | | 20 |
| | 60 | | 4 |

| | 10 | | 0 |
|---|---|---|---|
| | 0 | | 5 |
| | 3 | | 100 |
| | 16 | | 53 |

311

312

313

314

315

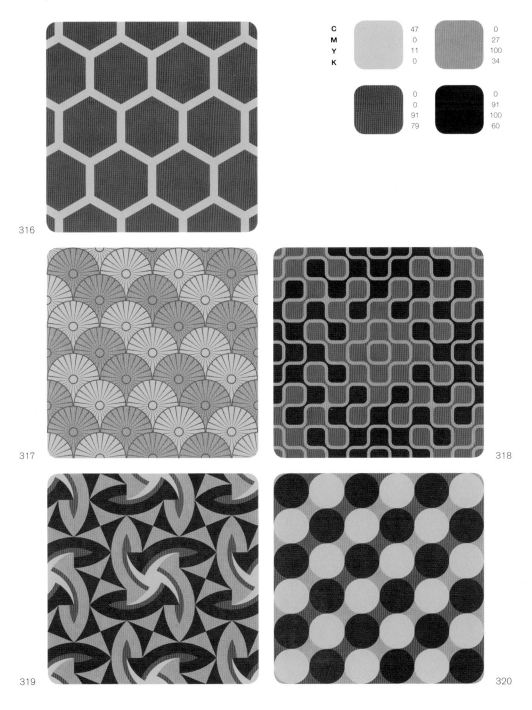

C 47 0
M 0 27
Y 11 100
K 0 34

0 0
0 91
91 100
79 60

316

317

318

319

320

# Color Moods

Color can evoke a positive or negative mood that can, in turn, increase sales, or calm a buyer in a retail setting. As designers, these are challenges we are faced with daily. When establishing a brand, we need to consider that all colors have meaning, and each one stimulates our senses in a different way. When selecting a palette, experiment with different hues to personalize the colors to your specific needs.

The colors in the following section are examples of powerful and successful color combinations that can quickly establish a mood.

| C | | | |
|---|---|---|---|
| **C** | 0 | 30 | |
| **M** | 100 | 56 | |
| **Y** | 79 | 100 | |
| **K** | 20 | 37 | |

| | | |
|---|---|---|
| 0 | 0 | |
| 5 | 97 | |
| 0 | 100 | |
| 100 | 50 | |

321

322

323

324

325

326

C 0 30
M 100 56
Y 79 100
K 20 37

0 14
5 0
0 10
100 6

0
97
100
50

327

328

329

330

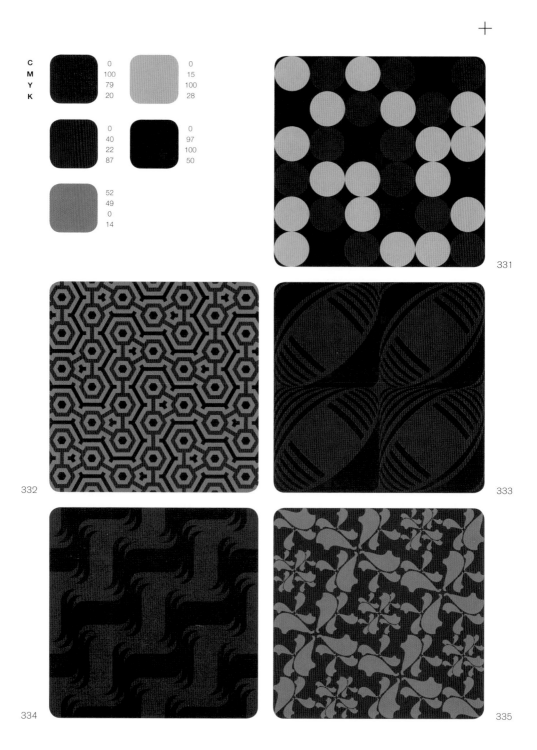

C 0  0
M 100  15
Y 79  100
K 20  28

0  0
40  97
22  100
87  50

52
49
0
14

331
332
333
334
335

336

C 0 0
M 100 24
Y 99 94
K 4 0

0
40
22
87

337

338

339

340

| | | | | | |
|---|---|---|---|---|---|
| C | 0 | | 0 | | |
| M | 100 | | 24 | | |
| Y | 99 | | 94 | | |
| K | 4 | | 0 | | |

| | | |
|---|---|---|
| 100 | 100 | |
| 0 | 0 | |
| 86 | 91 | |
| 3 | 42 | |

| | | |
|---|---|---|
| 100 | 0 | |
| 56 | 90 | |
| 0 | 100 | |
| 23 | 66 | |

347

348

349

350

**Color Moods** 81

| C | 0 | | 100 |
|---|---|---|---|
| M | 100 | | 0 |
| Y | 63 | | 9 |
| K | 29 | | 40 |

| | 100 | | 0 |
|---|---|---|---|
| | 68 | | 100 |
| | 0 | | 61 |
| | 52 | | 43 |

351

352

353

354

355

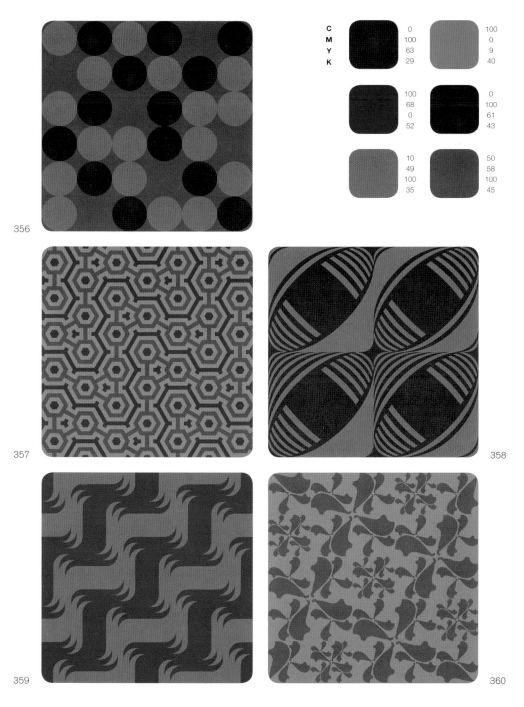

356

357

358

359

360

| | | |
|---|---|---|
| C | 0 | 100 |
| M | 100 | 0 |
| Y | 63 | 9 |
| K | 29 | 40 |
| | 100 | 0 |
| | 68 | 100 |
| | 0 | 61 |
| | 52 | 43 |
| | 10 | 50 |
| | 49 | 58 |
| | 100 | 100 |
| | 35 | 45 |

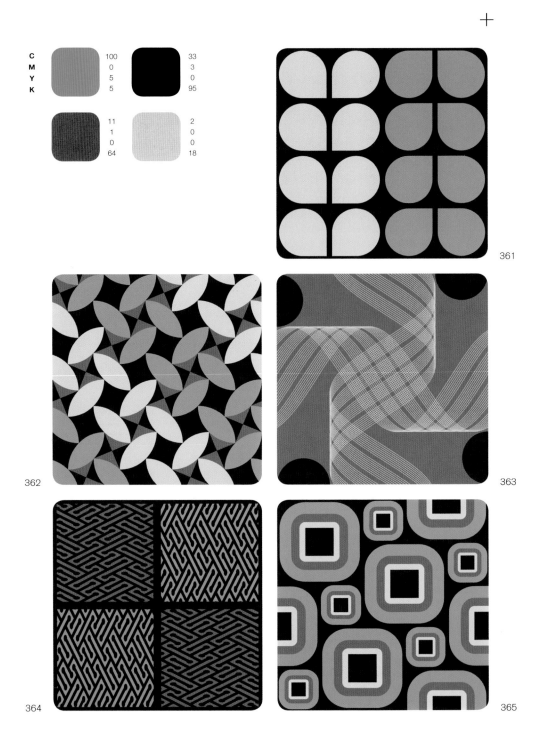

| | | |
|---|---|---|
| **C** | 100 | 33 |
| **M** | 0 | 3 |
| **Y** | 5 | 0 |
| **K** | 5 | 95 |

| | |
|---|---|
| 11 | 2 |
| 1 | 0 |
| 0 | 0 |
| 64 | 18 |

361

362

363

364

365

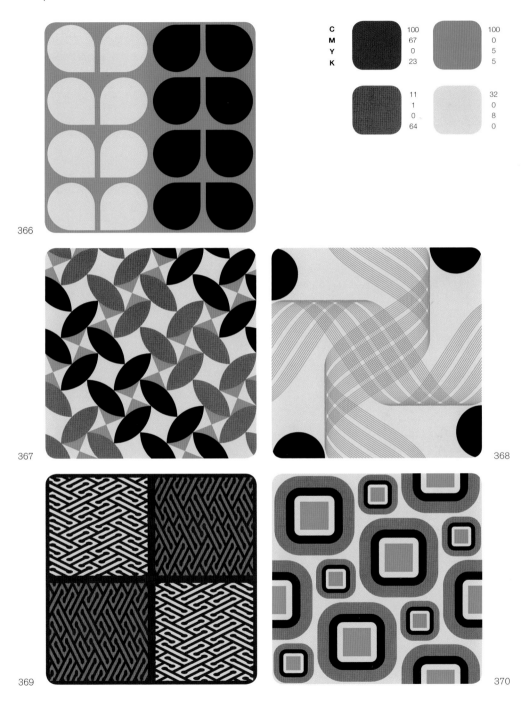

366

367

368

369

370

| C | 75 | | 50 |
|---|---|---|---|
| M | 0 | | 0 |
| Y | 7 | | 100 |
| K | 0 | | 0 |

| | 0 | | 0 |
|---|---|---|---|
| | 59 | | 28 |
| | 100 | | 100 |
| | 5 | | 6 |

| | 30 | | 0 |
|---|---|---|---|
| | 0 | | 9 |
| | 8 | | 58 |
| | 0 | | 0 |

371

372

373

374

375

376

377

378

379

380

The color swatches show:

C 0, M 59, Y 100, K 5
0, 9, 58, 0
30, 0, 8, 0
75, 0, 7, 0

**Color Moods** 87

381

382

383

384

385

386

| C | 100 | | 59 |
|---|-----|---|----|
| M | 0 | | 0 |
| Y | 71 | | 100 |
| K | 43 | | 7 |

| | 11 |
|---|----|
| | 0 |
| | 66 |
| | 2 |

387

388

389

390

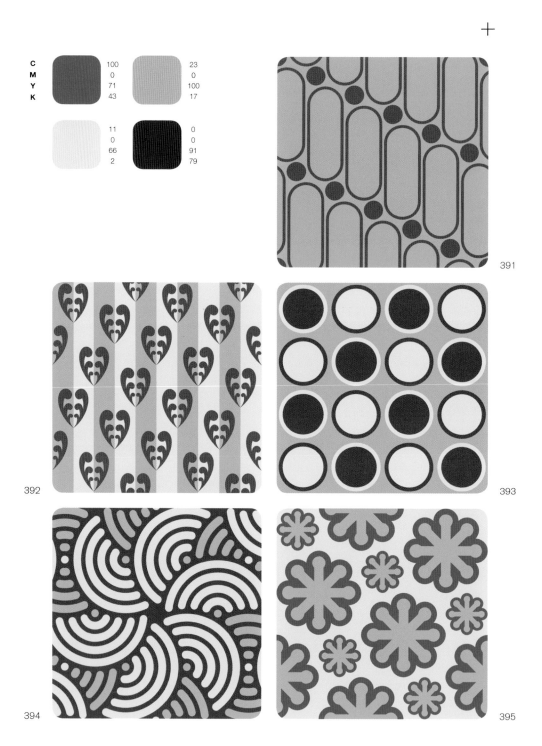

| C | 100 | | 23 |
|---|---|---|---|
| M | 0 | | 0 |
| Y | 71 | | 100 |
| K | 43 | | 17 |

| | 11 | | 0 |
|---|---|---|---|
| | 0 | | 0 |
| | 66 | | 91 |
| | 2 | | 79 |

391

392

393

394

395

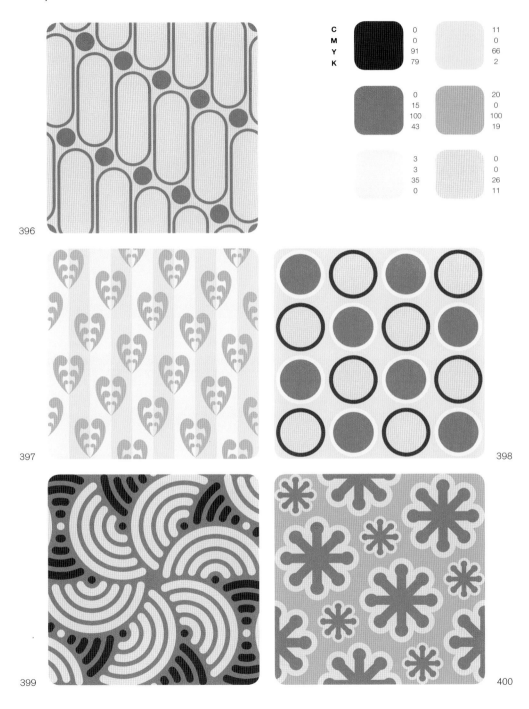

396

| | | | |
|---|---|---|---|
| **C** | 0 | | 11 |
| **M** | 0 | | 0 |
| **Y** | 91 | | 66 |
| **K** | 79 | | 2 |

| | | | |
|---|---|---|---|
| | 0 | | 20 |
| | 15 | | 0 |
| | 100 | | 100 |
| | 43 | | 19 |

| | | | |
|---|---|---|---|
| | 3 | | 0 |
| | 3 | | 0 |
| | 35 | | 26 |
| | 0 | | 11 |

397

398

399

400

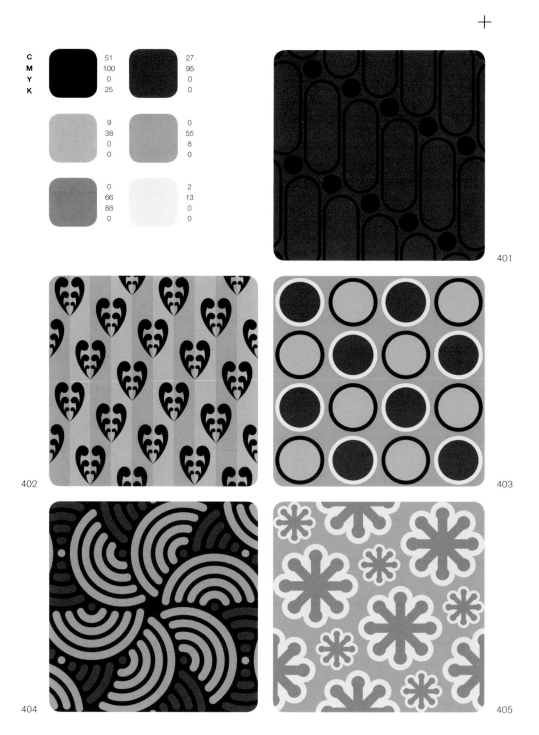

| | |
|---|---|
| **C** 51 | 27 |
| **M** 100 | 95 |
| **Y** 0 | 0 |
| **K** 25 | 0 |
| 9 | 0 |
| 38 | 55 |
| 0 | 8 |
| 0 | 0 |
| 0 | 2 |
| 66 | 13 |
| 88 | 0 |
| 0 | 0 |

401

402

403

404

405

| C | 51 | | 2 |
| M | 100 | | 13 |
| Y | 0 | | 0 |
| K | 25 | | 0 |

| | 10 | | 2 |
| | 1 | | 0 |
| | 0 | | 0 |
| | 40 | | 5 |

406

407

408

409

410

| C | 27 | | 2 |
|---|---|---|---|
| M | 95 | | 0 |
| Y | 0 | | 0 |
| K | 0 | | 5 |

| | 0 | | 0 |
|---|---|---|---|
| | 66 | | 100 |
| | 88 | | 63 |
| | 0 | | 12 |

411

412

413

414

415

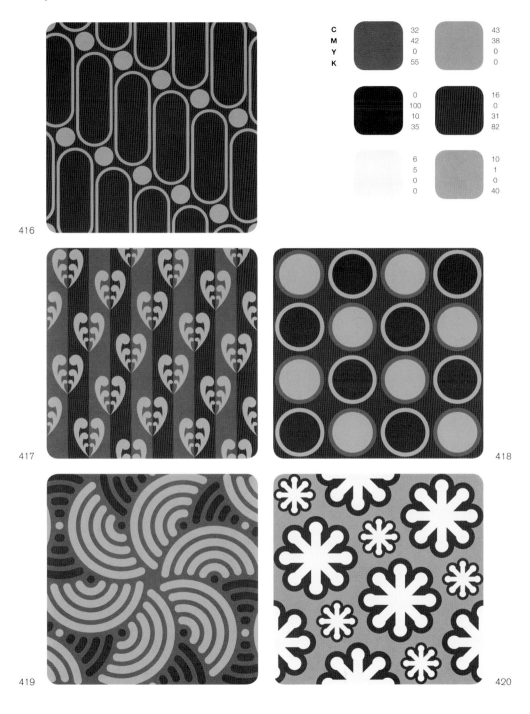

416

417

418

419

420

| | | |
|---|---|---|
| C | 32 | 43 |
| M | 42 | 38 |
| Y | 0 | 0 |
| K | 55 | 0 |

| | | |
|---|---|---|
| | 0 | 16 |
| | 100 | 0 |
| | 10 | 31 |
| | 35 | 82 |

| | | |
|---|---|---|
| | 6 | 10 |
| | 5 | 1 |
| | 0 | 0 |
| | 0 | 40 |

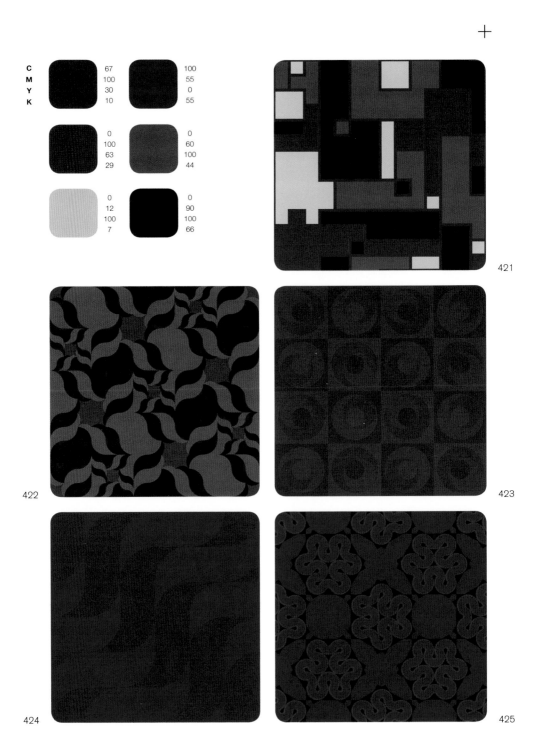

| | C | M | Y | K |
|---|---|---|---|---|
| | 67 | 100 | 30 | 10 |
| | 100 | 55 | 0 | 55 |
| | 0 | 100 | 63 | 29 |
| | 0 | 60 | 100 | 44 |
| | 0 | 12 | 100 | 7 |
| | 0 | 90 | 100 | 66 |

421

422

423

424

425

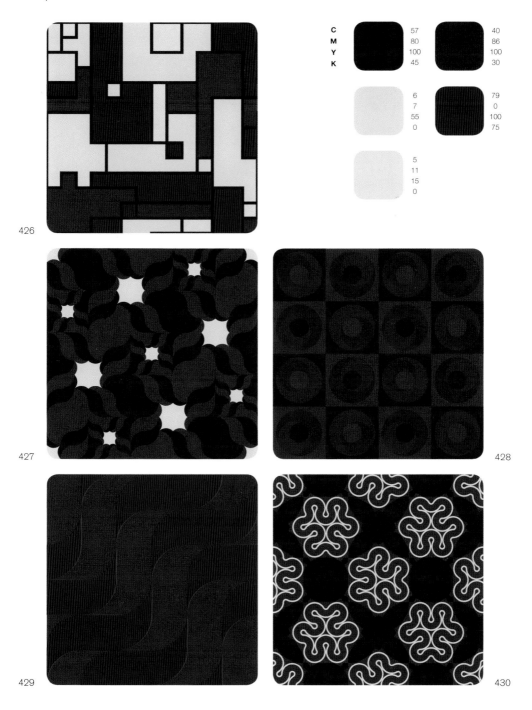

426

427

428

429

430

| | | |
|---|---|---|
| C | 57 | 40 |
| M | 80 | 86 |
| Y | 100 | 100 |
| K | 45 | 30 |
| | 6 | 79 |
| | 7 | 0 |
| | 55 | 100 |
| | 0 | 75 |
| | 5 | |
| | 11 | |
| | 15 | |
| | 0 | |

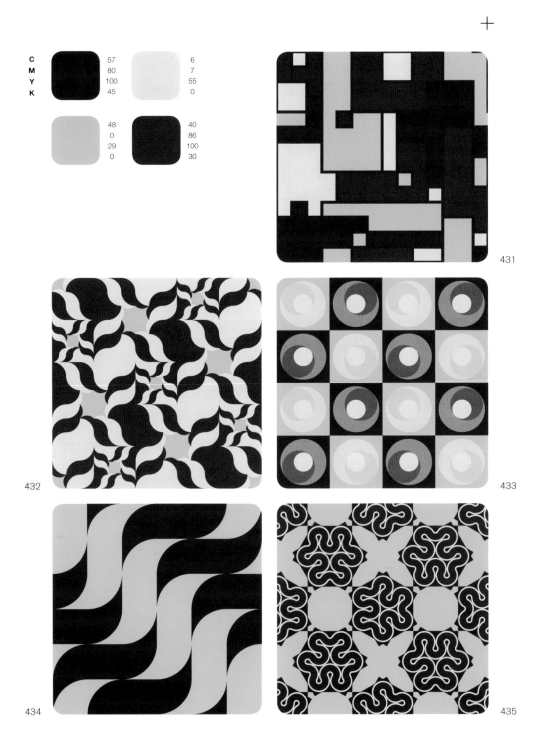

| C | 57 | | 6 |
|---|---|---|---|
| M | 80 | | 7 |
| Y | 100 | | 55 |
| K | 45 | | 0 |

| | 48 | | 40 |
|---|---|---|---|
| | 0 | | 86 |
| | 29 | | 100 |
| | 0 | | 30 |

431

432

433

434

435

436

437

438

439

440

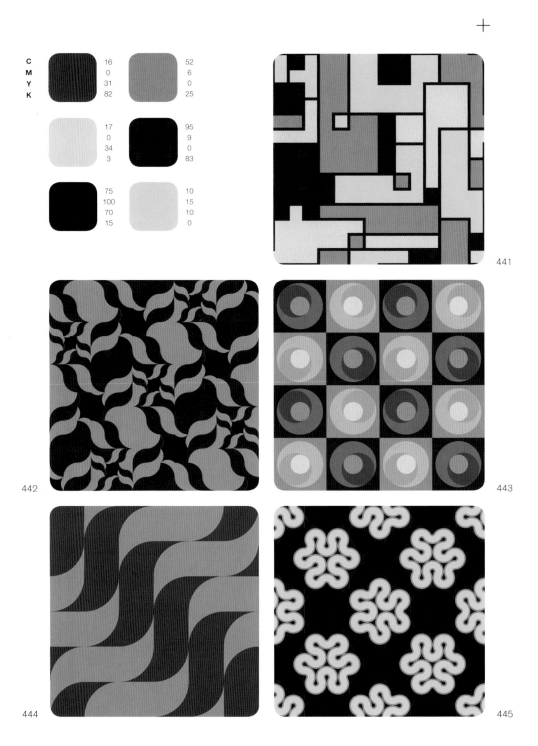

| | CMYK | |
|---|---|---|
| C | 16 | 52 |
| M | 0 | 6 |
| Y | 31 | 0 |
| K | 82 | 25 |
| | 17 | 95 |
| | 0 | 9 |
| | 34 | 0 |
| | 3 | 83 |
| | 75 | 10 |
| | 100 | 15 |
| | 70 | 10 |
| | 15 | 0 |

441

442

443

444

445

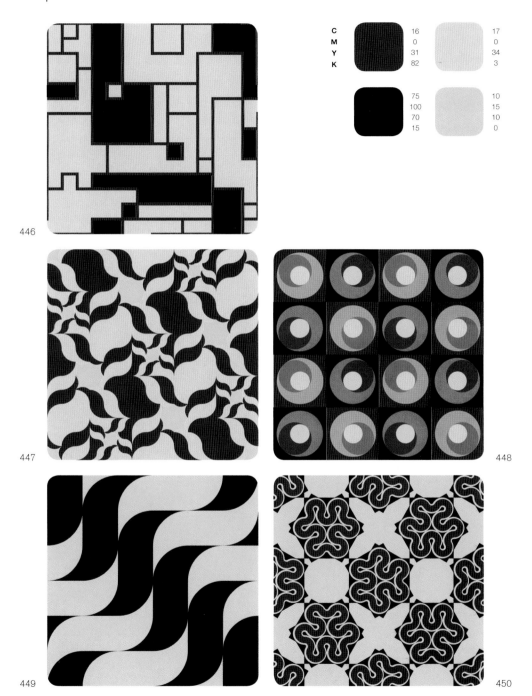

446

447

448

449

450

| | | |
|---|---|---|
| C | 16 | 17 |
| M | 0 | 0 |
| Y | 31 | 34 |
| K | 82 | 3 |
| C | 75 | 10 |
| M | 100 | 15 |
| Y | 70 | 10 |
| K | 15 | 0 |

| C | 52 | | 57 |
| M | 6 | | 80 |
| Y | 0 | | 100 |
| K | 25 | | 45 |
| | 20 | | 40 |
| | 0 | | 86 |
| | 40 | | 100 |
| | 6 | | 30 |

451

452

453

454

455

| C | | 30 | | 10 |
|---|---|---|---|---|
| M | | 0 | | 1 |
| Y | | 8 | | 0 |
| K | | 0 | | 40 |

|  | 6 |
|---|---|
|  | 5 |
|  | 0 |
|  | 0 |

456

457

458

459

460

| | | |
|---|---|---|
| **C** | | 0 | | 0 |
| **M** | | 59 | | 100 |
| **Y** | | 100 | | 63 |
| **K** | | 5 | | 29 |
| | | 0 | | 0 |
| | | 0 | | 12 |
| | | 26 | | 100 |
| | | 11 | | 7 |

461

462

463

464

465

466

| | | |
|---|---|---|
| C | 0 | 0 |
| M | 59 | 28 |
| Y | 100 | 100 |
| K | 5 | 6 |
| | 100 | 100 |
| | 67 | 0 |
| | 0 | 5 |
| | 23 | 5 |
| | 33 | 11 |
| | 3 | 1 |
| | 0 | 0 |
| | 95 | 64 |

467

468

469

470

| | | |
|---|---|---|
| C | 0 | 13 |
| M | 5 | 3 |
| Y | 0 | 0 |
| K | 100 | 17 |

| | |
|---|---|
| 100 | 100 |
| 5 | 0 |
| 0 | 5 |
| 47 | 5 |

| | |
|---|---|
| 10 | 6 |
| 1 | 5 |
| 0 | 0 |
| 40 | 0 |

471

472

473

474

475

| C | 57 | | 10 |
| M | 80 | | 1 |
| Y | 100 | | 0 |
| K | 45 | | 40 |

| | 20 | | 0 |
| | 0 | | 15 |
| | 40 | | 100 |
| | 6 | | 43 |

| | 0 |
| | 0 |
| | 26 |
| | 11 |

476

477

478

479

480

# Galaxy

Here is where art and science collide. Scientists and engineers often need to assign colors to visualize an object that would not ordinarily be visible to the human eye or to bring out subtle details.

Therefore, in science, we usually see dark shades paired with primary colors and neon. Looking at images under a microscope or through a telescope are great ways to get inspired.

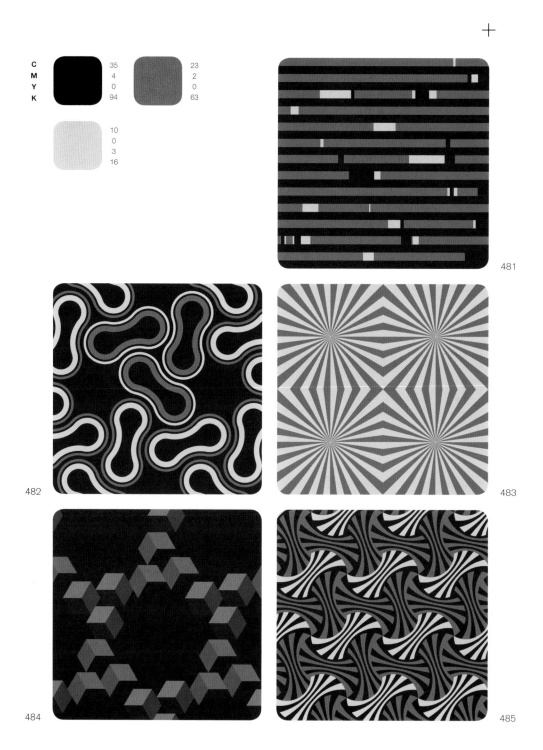

C  
M  
Y  
K

35  
4  
0  
94

23  
2  
0  
63

10  
0  
3  
16

481

482

483

484

485

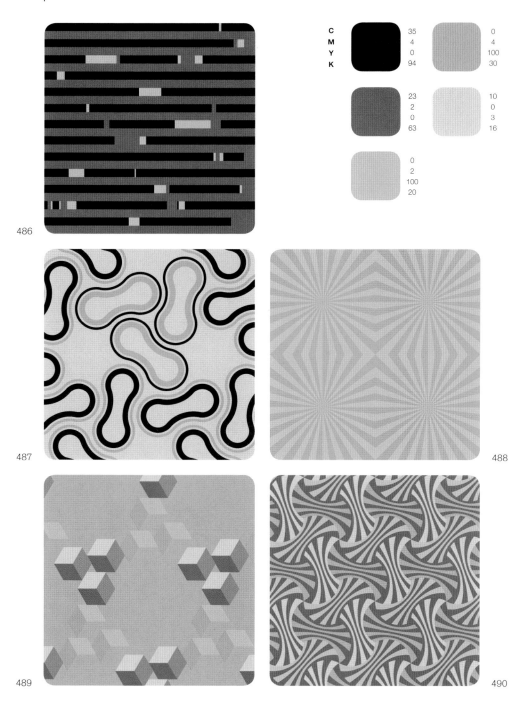

486

| | | |
|---|---|---|
| C | 35 | 0 |
| M | 4 | 4 |
| Y | 0 | 100 |
| K | 94 | 30 |

| 23 | 10 |
|---|---|
| 2 | 0 |
| 0 | 3 |
| 63 | 16 |

| 0 |
|---|
| 2 |
| 100 |
| 20 |

487

488

489

490

C
M
Y
K

| 0 | 0 |
| 0 | 0 |
| 0 | 0 |
| 99 | 44 |

| 62 | 100 |
| 22 | 57 |
| 0 | 0 |
| 3 | 38 |

| 22 |
| 3 |
| 0 |
| 0 |

491

492

493

194

495

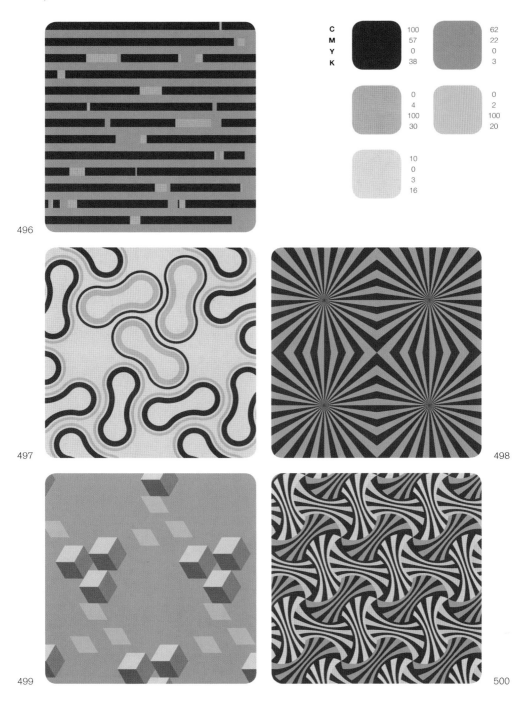

C 100
M 57
Y 0
K 38

62
22
0
3

0
4
100
30

0
2
100
20

10
0
3
16

496

497

498

499

500

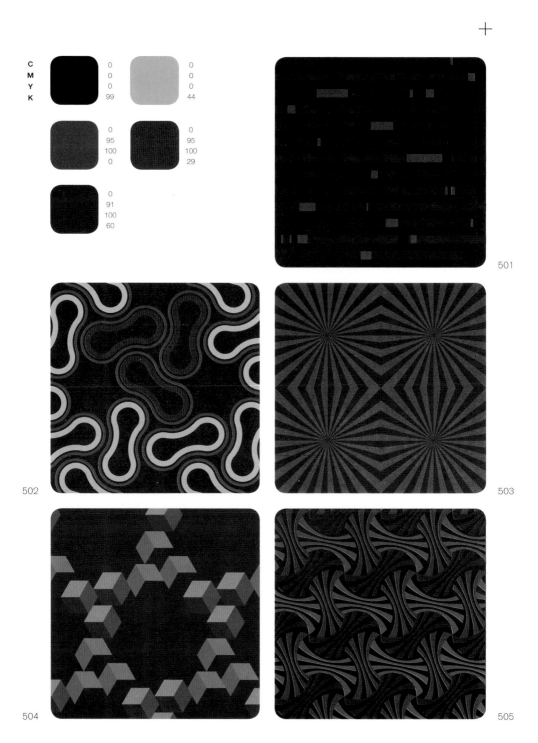

| | | |
|---|---|---|
| C | 0 | 0 |
| M | 0 | 0 |
| Y | 0 | 0 |
| K | 99 | 44 |

| | |
|---|---|
| 0 | 0 |
| 95 | 95 |
| 100 | 100 |
| 0 | 29 |

| |
|---|
| 0 |
| 91 |
| 100 |
| 60 |

501

502

503

504

505

506

| | C | 0 | | 0 |
|---|---|---|---|---|
| | M | 91 | | 95 |
| | Y | 100 | | 100 |
| | K | 60 | | 29 |

| | 0 | | 0 |
|---|---|---|---|
| | 4 | | 2 |
| | 100 | | 100 |
| | 30 | | 20 |

| | 35 | | 10 |
|---|---|---|---|
| | 4 | | 0 |
| | 0 | | 3 |
| | 94 | | 16 |

507

508

509

510

| | | |
|---|---|---|
| C | 35 | 0 |
| M | 4 | 95 |
| Y | 0 | 100 |
| K | 94 | 0 |

| | |
|---|---|
| 62 | |
| 22 | |
| 0 | |
| 3 | |

511

512

513

514

515

516

517

518

519

520

| C | 100 | | 100 |
|---|---|---|---|
| M | 11 | | 44 |
| Y | 0 | | 0 |
| K | 74 | | 0 |

| | 30 | | 0 |
|---|---|---|---|
| | 0 | | 91 |
| | 5 | | 100 |
| | 0 | | 23 |

| | 0 | | 0 |
|---|---|---|---|
| | 30 | | 46 |
| | 95 | | 100 |
| | 0 | | 11 |

521

522

523

524

525

526

527

528

529

530

C 0 0
M 91 30
Y 100 95
K 23 0

100 0
11 91
0 100
74 60

| | C | 80 | | 65 |
| | M | 0 | | 0 |
| | Y | 63 | | 56 |
| | K | 75 | | 94 |

| | 88 | | 0 |
| | 0 | | 0 |
| | 57 | | 25 |
| | 36 | | 13 |

| | 0 |
| | 0 |
| | 20 |
| | 4 |

531

532

533

534

535

C 65
M 0
Y 56
K 94

88
0
57
36

0
0
20
4

536

537

538

539

540

546

547

548

549

550

| C | 72 | | 0 |
|---|----|---|---|
| M | 90 | | 32 |
| Y | 75 | | 100 |
| K | 15 | | 9 |

| | 7 | | 46 |
|---|---|---|---|
| | 9 | | 45 |
| | 10 | | 49 |
| | 0 | | 0 |

| C | 0 | | 10 |
| M | 0 | | 0 |
| Y | 91 | | 3 |
| K | 79 | | 16 |

| | 0 | | 46 |
| | 2 | | 45 |
| | 87 | | 49 |
| | 59 | | 0 |

551

552

553

554

555

556

| C | 35 | 72 |
| M | 4 | 90 |
| Y | 0 | 75 |
| K | 94 | 15 |

| | 46 | 10 |
| | 45 | 0 |
| | 49 | 3 |
| | 0 | 16 |

| | 0 | |
| | 32 | |
| | 100 | |
| | 9 | |

557

558

559

560

| C | 0 | | 0 |
|---|---|---|---|
| M | 70 | | 58 |
| Y | 100 | | 100 |
| K | 78 | | 49 |

| | 36 | | 58 |
|---|---|---|---|
| | 0 | | 0 |
| | 49 | | 80 |
| | 0 | | 0 |

561

562

563

564

565

| | | | | | | |
|---|---|---|---|---|---|---|
| **C** | 58 | 0 | | | | |
| **M** | 0 | 43 | | | | |
| **Y** | 80 | 100 | | | | |
| **K** | 0 | 33 | | | | |

566

567

568

569

570

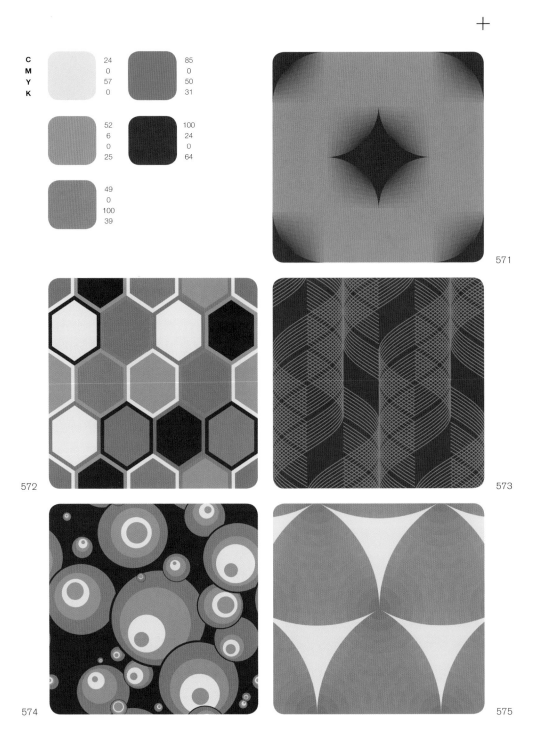

| C | 24 | | 85 |
|---|---|---|---|
| M | 0 | | 0 |
| Y | 57 | | 50 |
| K | 0 | | 31 |

| | 52 | | 100 |
|---|---|---|---|
| | 6 | | 24 |
| | 0 | | 0 |
| | 25 | | 64 |

| | 49 |
|---|---|
| | 0 |
| | 100 |
| | 39 |

571

572

573

574

575

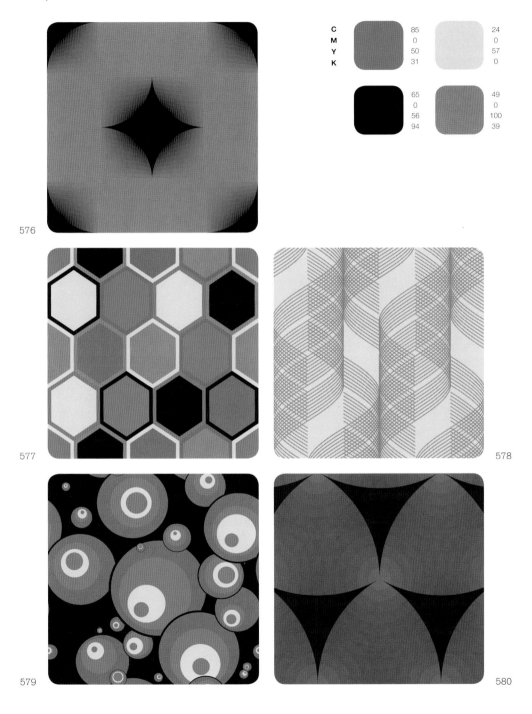

| | | | |
|---|---|---|---|
| C | 85 | | 24 |
| M | 0 | | 0 |
| Y | 50 | | 57 |
| K | 31 | | 0 |
| | 65 | | 49 |
| | 0 | | 0 |
| | 56 | | 100 |
| | 94 | | 39 |

576

577

578

579

580

| | | | |
|---|---|---|---|
| C | 100 | | 30 |
| M | 11 | | 0 |
| Y | 0 | | 5 |
| K | 74 | | 0 |
| | 58 | | 100 |
| | 0 | | 44 |
| | 80 | | 0 |
| | 0 | | 0 |
| | 35 | | 10 |
| | 4 | | 0 |
| | 0 | | 3 |
| | 94 | | 16 |

581

582

583

584

585

| C | 0 | | 0 |
|---|---|---|---|
| M | 14 | | 5 |
| Y | 28 | | 10 |
| K | 55 | | 29 |

| | 0 | | 0 |
|---|---|---|---|
| | 32 | | 0 |
| | 100 | | 20 |
| | 9 | | 4 |

586

587

588

589

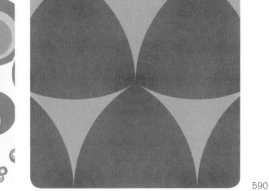

590

C 0 0
M 14 4
Y 28 100
K 55 30

62 22
22 3
0 0
3 0

591

592

593

594

595

C 0
M 14
Y 28
K 55

0
95
100
29

7
9
10
0

0
70
100
78

596

597

598

599

600

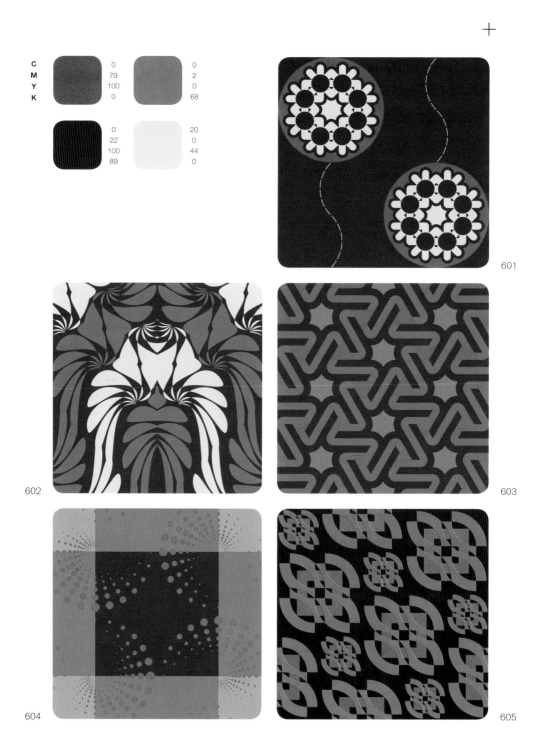

| C | | 0 | | 0 |
|---|---|---|---|---|
| M | | 79 | | 2 |
| Y | | 100 | | 0 |
| K | | 0 | | 68 |

| | 0 | | 20 |
|---|---|---|---|
| | 22 | | 0 |
| | 100 | | 44 |
| | 89 | | 0 |

601

602

603

604

605

606

607

608

609

610

| | | |
|---|---|---|
| C | 0 | 100 |
| M | 0 | 73 |
| Y | 0 | 0 |
| K | 100 | 2 |
| | 0 | 6 |
| | 91 | 0 |
| | 100 | 28 |
| | 23 | 27 |

611

612

613

614

615

616

| | | |
|---|---|---|
| C | 0 | 61 |
| M | 0 | 89 |
| Y | 0 | 0 |
| K | 100 | 0 |

| 30 | 29 |
|---|---|
| 56 | 36 |
| 100 | 0 |
| 37 | 0 |

| 0 |
|---|
| 0 |
| 31 |
| 18 |

617

618

619

620

| | | | |
|---|---|---|---|
| C | 61 | | 29 |
| M | 89 | | 36 |
| Y | 0 | | 0 |
| K | 0 | | 0 |
| | 0 | | 30 |
| | 0 | | 56 |
| | 31 | | 100 |
| | 18 | | 37 |
| | 20 | | 0 |
| | 32 | | 100 |
| | 58 | | 43 |
| | 0 | | 19 |

621

622

623

624

625

626

C 22 100
M 3 44
Y 0 0
K 0 0

0 0
58 32
100 100
10 9

0 0
14 5
28 10
55 29

627

628

629

630

| | | |
|---|---|---|
| C | 65 | 88 |
| M | 0 | 0 |
| Y | 56 | 57 |
| K | 94 | 36 |
| | 80 | 100 |
| | 0 | 73 |
| | 63 | 0 |
| | 75 | 2 |
| | 0 | 0 |
| | 2 | 4 |
| | 100 | 100 |
| | 20 | 30 |

631

632

633

634

635

636

637

638

639

640

# Reinventing

Diversifying yourself from the competition is what it's all about. The following examples will help you move from traditional to contemporary. Thanks to the newest technology, we can pair just about any color combination with green to make an ecofriendly environment.

Appealing to a new generation of consumers can be very lucrative. Consider gender, age, location, or ethnic differences in your audience when making significant changes to an existing brand.

| | | | |
|---|---|---|---|
| **C** | 10 | | 0 |
| **M** | 0 | | 91 |
| **Y** | 3 | | 76 |
| **K** | 16 | | 0 |

| | |
|---|---|
| | 0 |
| | 4 |
| | 30 |
| | 11 |

641

642

643

644

645

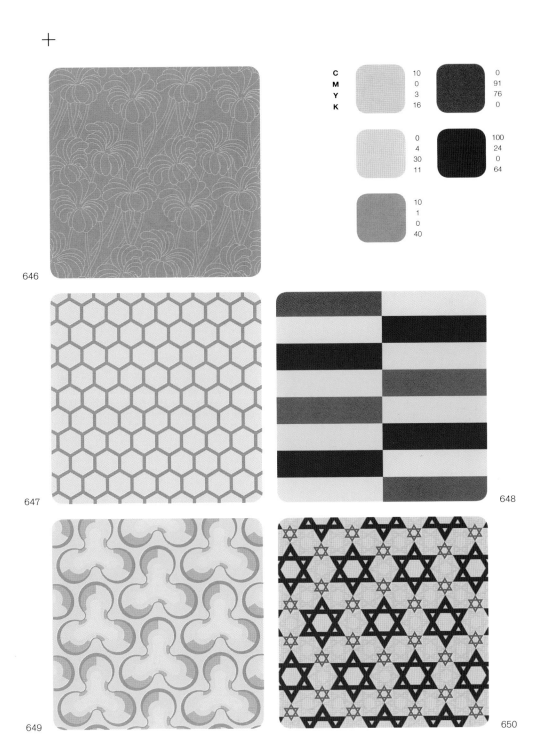

646

| | C | M | Y | K |
|---|---|---|---|---|
| | 10 | 0 | 3 | 16 |
| | 0 | 91 | 76 | 0 |
| | 0 | 4 | 30 | 11 |
| | 100 | 24 | 0 | 64 |
| | 10 | 1 | 0 | 40 |

647

648

649

650

| | | | |
|---|---|---|---|
| **C** | 60 | 30 | |
| **M** | 80 | 30 | |
| **Y** | 80 | 50 | |
| **K** | 15 | 35 | |

| | |
|---|---|
| | 0 |
| | 100 |
| | 90 |
| | 10 |

651

652

653

654

655

C 60
M 80
Y 80
K 15

30
30
50
35

15
0
10
0

656

657

658

659

660

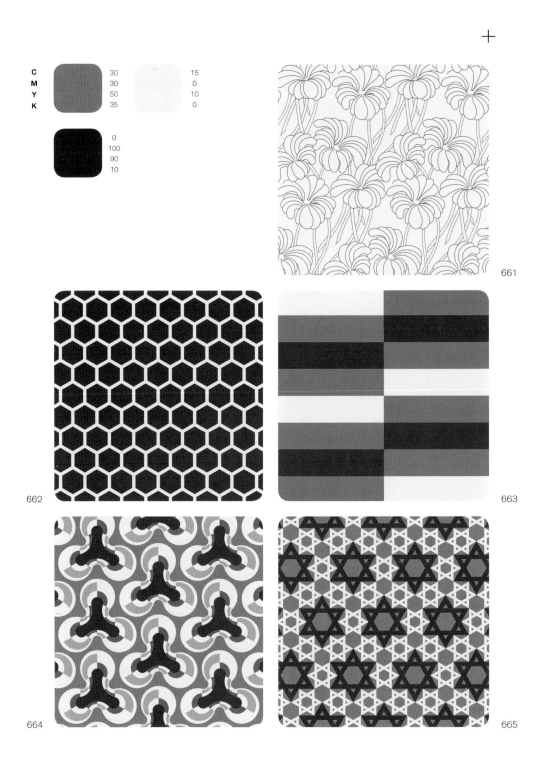

| C | 30 | | 15 |
|---|-----|---|-----|
| M | 30 | | 0 |
| Y | 50 | | 10 |
| K | 35 | | 0 |

| C | 0 |
|---|-----|
| M | 100 |
| Y | 90 |
| K | 10 |

661

662

663

664

665

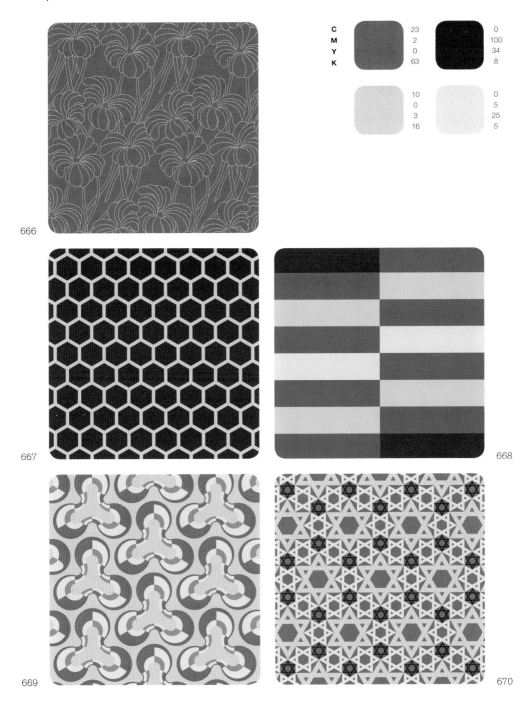

| | | | | |
|---|---|---|---|---|
| C | 23 | | 0 | |
| M | 2 | | 100 | |
| Y | 0 | | 34 | |
| K | 63 | | 8 | |
| | 10 | | 0 | |
| | 0 | | 5 | |
| | 3 | | 25 | |
| | 16 | | 5 | |

666

667

668

669

670

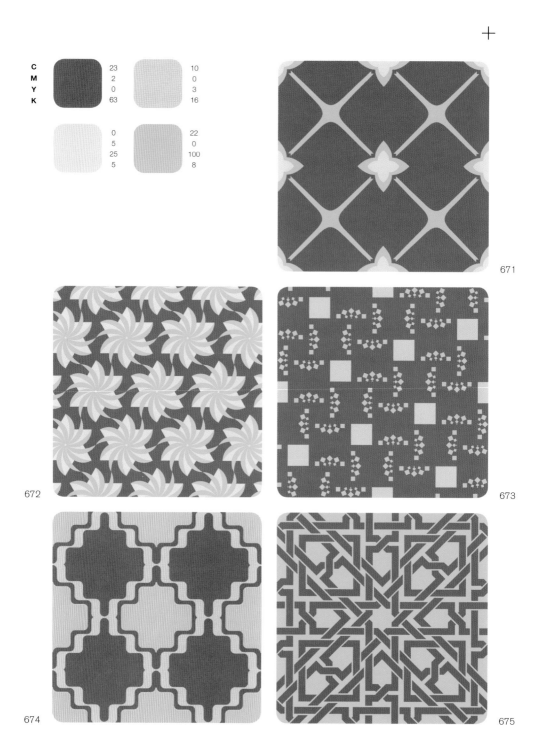

| C | | 23 | | 10 |
|---|---|---|---|---|
| M | | 2 | | 0 |
| Y | | 0 | | 3 |
| K | | 63 | | 16 |

| | 0 | | 22 |
|---|---|---|---|
| | 5 | | 0 |
| | 25 | | 100 |
| | 5 | | 8 |

671

672

673

674

675

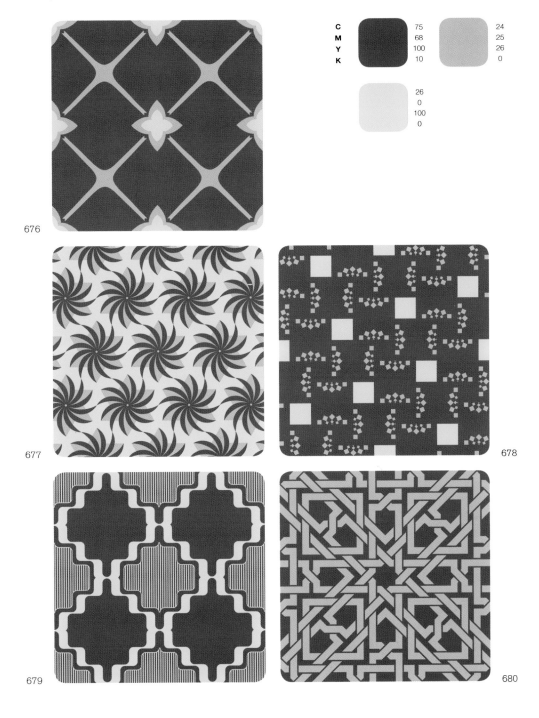

| | | |
|---|---|---|
| C | 75 | 24 |
| M | 68 | 25 |
| Y | 100 | 26 |
| K | 10 | 0 |

| | |
|---|---|
| | 26 |
| | 0 |
| | 100 |
| | 0 |

676

677

678

679

680

| C | 65 | 100 |
|---|----|-----|
| M | 30 | 60 |
| Y | 30 | 50 |
| K | 40 | 40 |

| 13 |
|----|
| 0 |
| 72 |
| 0 |

681

682

683

684

685

| C | M | Y | K |
|---|---|---|---|
| 30 | 30 | 50 | 35 |
| 13 | 0 | 72 | 0 |
| 10 | 0 | 3 | 16 |
| 60 | 80 | 80 | 15 |

686

687

688

689

690

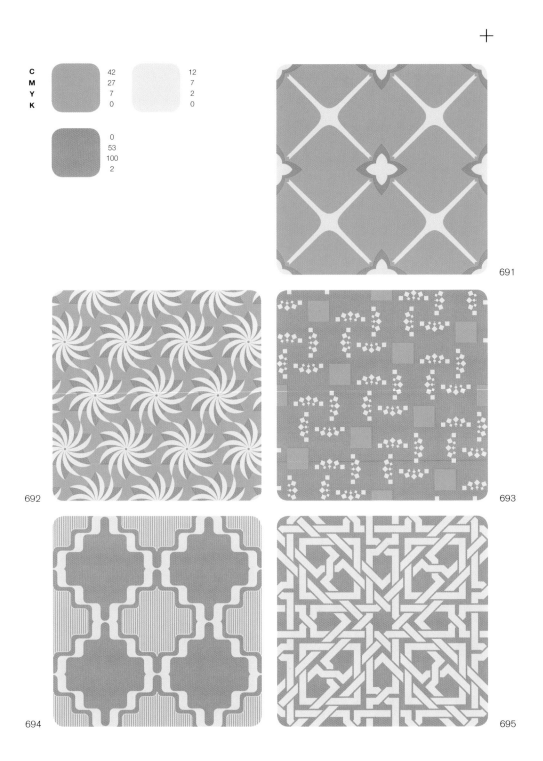

| C | 42 | | 12 |
|---|----|--|----|
| M | 27 | | 7 |
| Y | 7 | | 2 |
| K | 0 | | 0 |

| 0 |
|---|
| 53 |
| 100 |
| 2 |

691

692

693

694

695

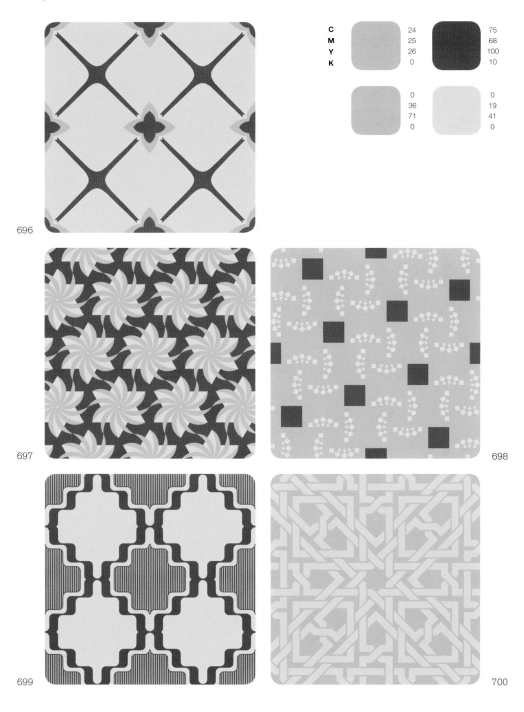

| C | | 24 | | 75 |
|---|---|---|---|---|
| M | | 25 | | 68 |
| Y | | 26 | | 100 |
| K | | 0 | | 10 |

| | 0 | | 0 |
|---|---|---|---|
| | 36 | | 19 |
| | 71 | | 41 |
| | 0 | | 0 |

696

697

698

699

700

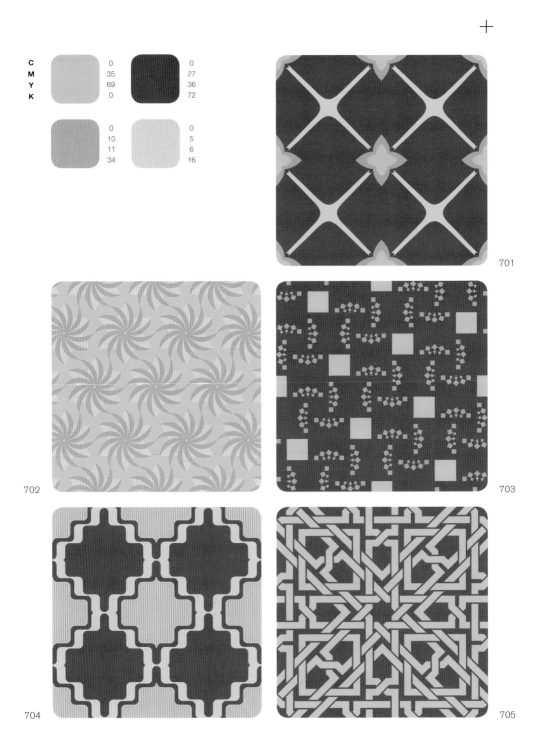

| | | |
|---|---|---|
| **C** | 0 | 0 |
| **M** | 35 | 27 |
| **Y** | 69 | 36 |
| **K** | 0 | 72 |
| | 0 | 0 |
| | 10 | 5 |
| | 11 | 6 |
| | 34 | 16 |

701

702

703

704

705

706

C 60 30
M 80 30
Y 80 50
K 15 35

10 0
0 35
3 69
16 0

707

708

709

710

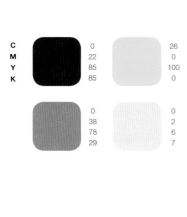

| | | |
|---|---|---|
| C | 0 | 26 |
| M | 22 | 0 |
| Y | 85 | 100 |
| K | 85 | 0 |
| | 0 | 0 |
| | 38 | 2 |
| | 78 | 6 |
| | 29 | 7 |

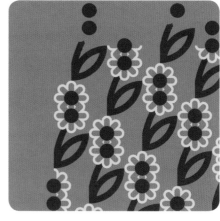

711

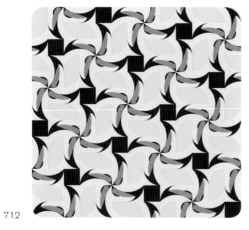

712

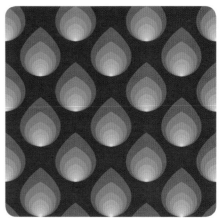

713

714

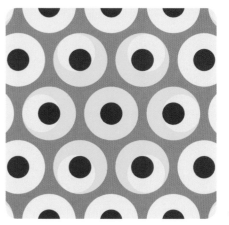

715

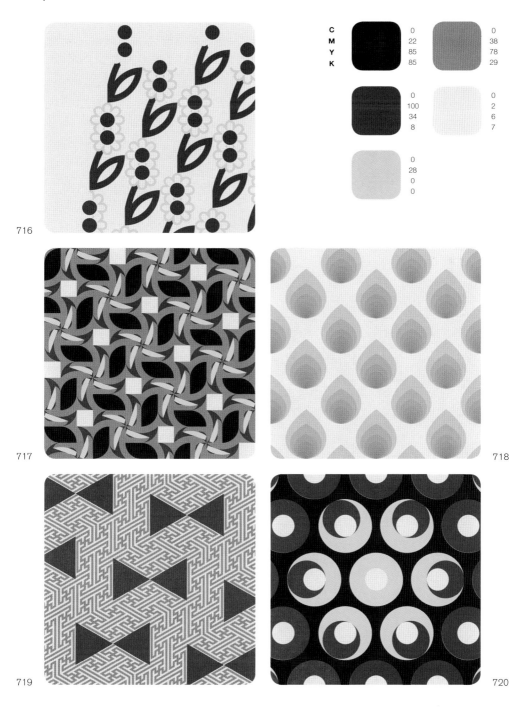

716

717

718

C 0 0
M 22 38
Y 85 78
K 85 29

0 0
100 2
34 6
8 7

0
28
0
0

719

720

| | |
|---|---|
| C | 75 |
| M | 68 |
| Y | 100 |
| K | 10 |

| 24 |
| 25 |
| 26 |
| 0 |

| 0 |
| 16 |
| 77 |
| 0 |

727

728

729

730

Reinventing 161

| C | 0 | | 23 |
|---|---|---|---|
| M | 40 | | 2 |
| Y | 22 | | 0 |
| K | 87 | | 63 |

| | 10 | | 0 |
|---|---|---|---|
| | 0 | | 16 |
| | 3 | | 77 |
| | 16 | | 0 |

731

732

733

734

735

C
M
Y
K

| | 0 | | 0 |
| | 22 | | 38 |
| | 85 | | 78 |
| | 85 | | 29 |

| | 0 | | 13 |
| | 2 | | 0 |
| | 6 | | 72 |
| | 7 | | 0 |

737

738

739

740

| | | |
|---|---|---|
| C | 100 | 24 |
| M | 35 | 25 |
| Y | 0 | 26 |
| K | 100 | 0 |

| | |
|---|---|
| 67 | |
| 2 | |
| 12 | |
| 2 | |

741

742

743

744

745

746

| | | | |
|---|---|---|---|
| C | 100 | | 24 |
| M | 35 | | 25 |
| Y | 0 | | 26 |
| K | 100 | | 0 |

| | | |
|---|---|---|
| 13 | | 0 |
| 15 | | 100 |
| 15 | | 99 |
| 0 | | 4 |

747

748

749

750

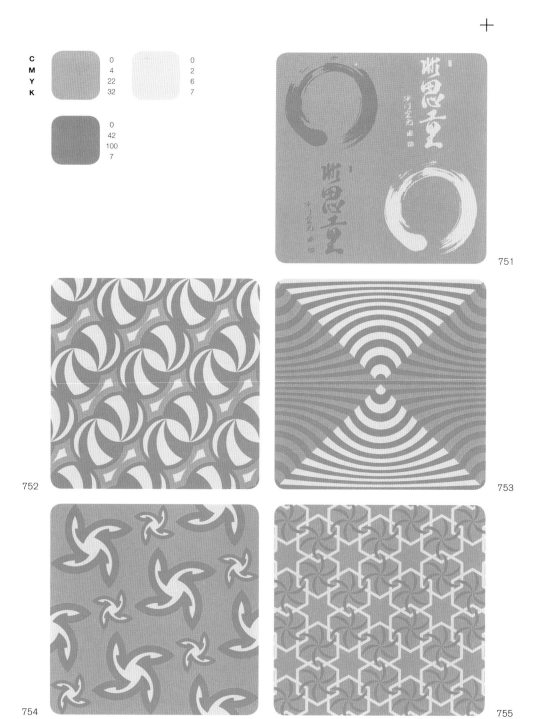

| C | 0 | | 0 |
|---|---|---|---|
| M | 4 | | 2 |
| Y | 22 | | 6 |
| K | 32 | | 7 |

| | 0 |
|---|---|
| | 42 |
| | 100 |
| | 7 |

751

752

753

754

755

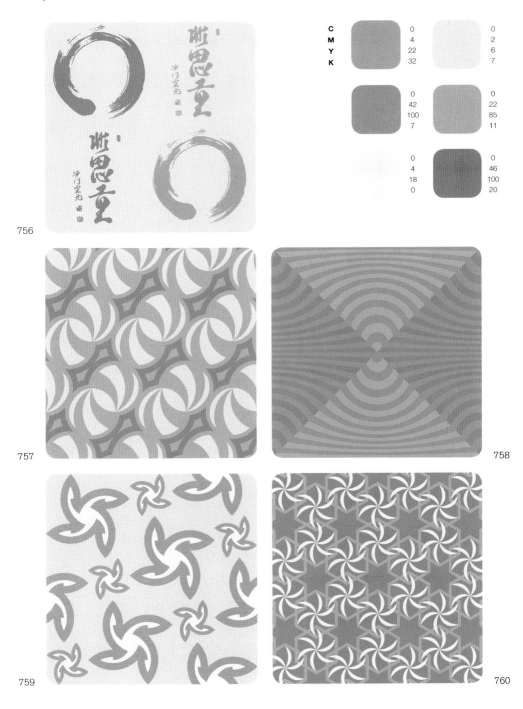

756

| C | 0 | | 0 |
|---|---|---|---|
| M | 4 | | 2 |
| Y | 22 | | 6 |
| K | 32 | | 7 |

| | 0 | | 0 |
|---|---|---|---|
| | 42 | | 22 |
| | 100 | | 85 |
| | 7 | | 11 |

| | 0 | | 0 |
|---|---|---|---|
| | 4 | | 46 |
| | 18 | | 100 |
| | 0 | | 20 |

757

758

759

760

| | | | | |
|---|---|---|---|---|
| **C** | 9 | **C** | 20 | |
| **M** | 6 | **M** | 32 | |
| **Y** | 17 | **Y** | 58 | |
| **K** | 0 | **K** | 0 | |

| | |
|---|---|
| **C** | 0 |
| **M** | 1 |
| **Y** | 0 |
| **K** | 43 |

761

762

763

764

765

766

| | C | 0 | | 0 |
| | M | 0 | | 0 |
| | Y | 0 | | 0 |
| | K | 100 | | 29 |

| 6 |
| 9 |
| 23 |
| 0 |

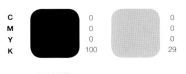

767

768

769

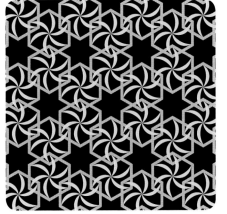

770

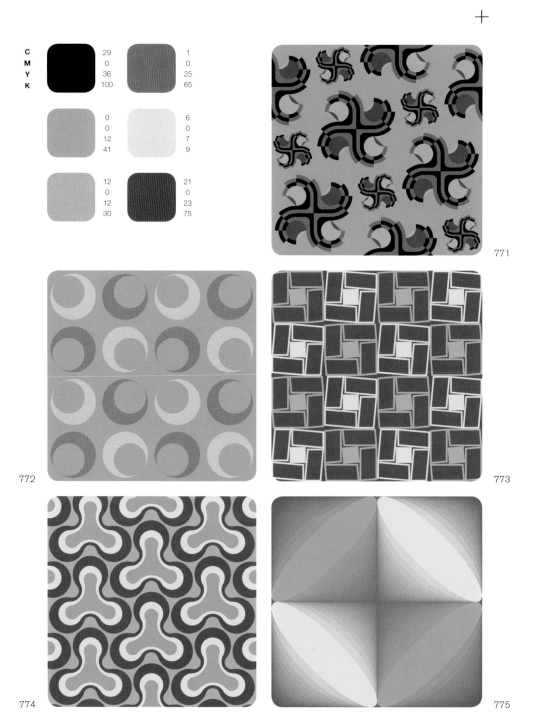

| | | |
|---|---|---|
| C | 29 | 1 |
| M | 0 | 0 |
| Y | 36 | 25 |
| K | 100 | 65 |
| | 0 | 6 |
| | 0 | 0 |
| | 12 | 7 |
| | 41 | 9 |
| | 12 | 21 |
| | 0 | 0 |
| | 12 | 23 |
| | 30 | 75 |

771

772

773

774

775

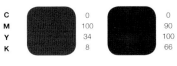

| | | |
|---|---|---|
| C | | 0 |
| M | | 100 |
| Y | | 34 |
| K | | 8 |

| | |
|---|---|
| | 0 |
| | 90 |
| | 100 |
| | 66 |

| | |
|---|---|
| | 12 |
| | 22 |
| | 43 |
| | 0 |

776

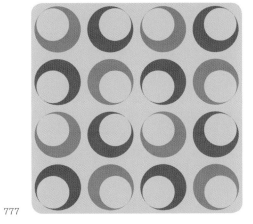

777

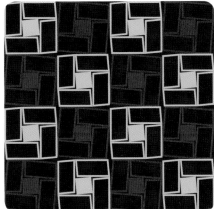

778

779

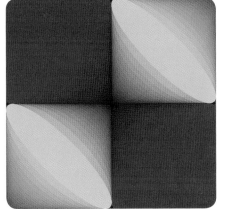

780

| C | 0 | | 0 |
|---|---|---|---|
| M | 100 | | 90 |
| Y | 34 | | 100 |
| K | 8 | | 66 |

| | 12 | | 0 |
|---|---|---|---|
| | 22 | | 0 |
| | 43 | | 0 |
| | 0 | | 100 |

| | 0 |
|---|---|
| | 0 |
| | 0 |
| | 29 |

781

782

783

784

785

C 0    24
M 2    25
Y 5    26
K 9    0

10    0
0    36
49    100
28    63

787

788

789

790

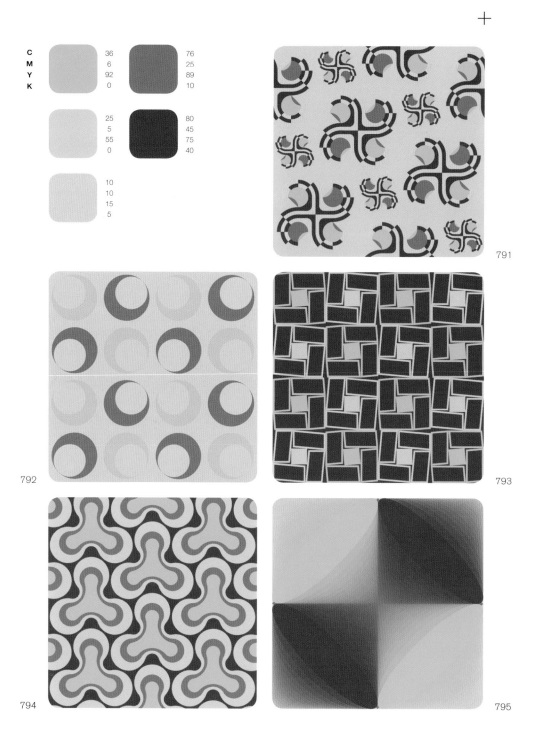

| | | |
|---|---|---|
| C | 36 | 76 |
| M | 6 | 25 |
| Y | 92 | 89 |
| K | 0 | 10 |
| | 25 | 80 |
| | 5 | 45 |
| | 55 | 75 |
| | 0 | 40 |
| | 10 | |
| | 10 | |
| | 15 | |
| | 5 | |

791

792

793

794

795

796

| | |
|---|---|
| C 15 | 25 |
| M 30 | 10 |
| Y 45 | 10 |
| K 5 | 0 |

| 5 | 30 |
|---|---|
| 75 | 15 |
| 95 | 5 |
| 0 | 0 |

| 0 | 15 |
|---|---|
| 25 | 10 |
| 40 | 75 |
| 0 | 0 |

797

798

799

800

# Globe-trotter

In this chapter we explore new trends in travel; hotels, restaurants, and retail. Warm neutrals have been the palette of choice for more than a decade. The earth-friendly movement is driving what's stylish, pairing these tired neutrals with bursts of fuchsia, green, and yellow, launching them into the present.

Neutrals are changing as well; gray is the new beige. Neutral blue shades evoke a sense of optimism. The new neutrals have a much cooler cast and work well at creating a strong sense of calm.

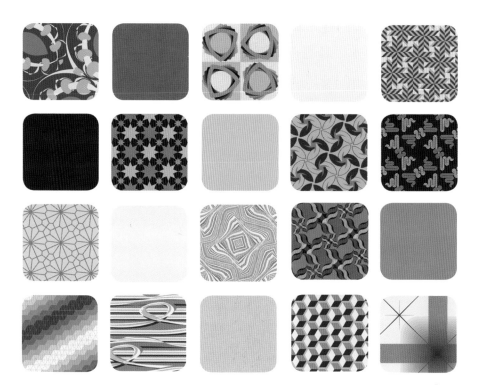

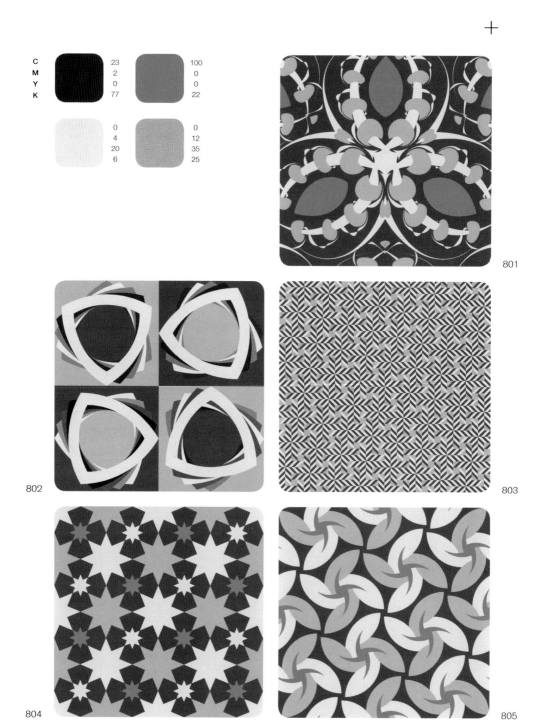

| C | 23 | | 100 |
|---|---|---|---|
| M | 2 | | 0 |
| Y | 0 | | 0 |
| K | 77 | | 22 |

| | 0 | | 0 |
|---|---|---|---|
| | 4 | | 12 |
| | 20 | | 35 |
| | 6 | | 25 |

801

802

803

804

805

806

| | | | | | |
|---|---|---|---|---|---|
| C | 100 | | 0 | | |
| M | 0 | | 55 | | |
| Y | 0 | | 100 | | |
| K | 22 | | 64 | | |

| | |
|---|---|
| 0 | 0 |
| 12 | 38 |
| 35 | 78 |
| 25 | 29 |

| | |
|---|---|
| 0 | 0 |
| 8 | 3 |
| 21 | 10 |
| 32 | 10 |

807

808

809

810

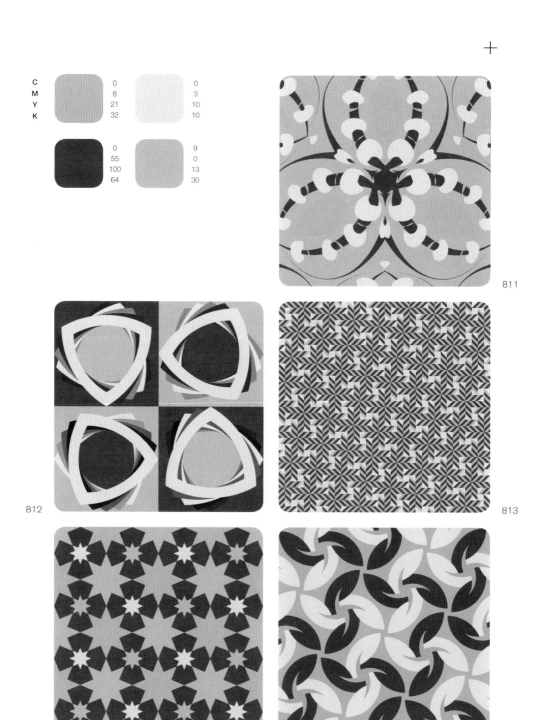

| | C | 0 | | 0 |
|---|---|---|---|---|
| | M | 8 | | 3 |
| | Y | 21 | | 10 |
| | K | 32 | | 10 |
| | | 0 | | 9 |
| | | 55 | | 0 |
| | | 100 | | 13 |
| | | 64 | | 30 |

811

812

813

814

815

816

817

818

819

820

| C | 0 | | 0 |
| M | 22 | | 12 |
| Y | 85 | | 35 |
| K | 85 | | 25 |

| C | 98 |
| M | 0 |
| Y | 57 |
| K | 17 |

821

822

823

824

825

826

| C | 23 | | 0 |
| M | 2 | | 55 |
| Y | 0 | | 100 |
| K | 77 | | 64 |

| | 0 | | 0 |
| | 8 | | 3 |
| | 21 | | 10 |
| | 32 | | 10 |

| | 1 |
| | 70 |
| | 100 |
| | 7 |

827

828

829

830

C 30
M 6
Y 0
K 0

38
4
0
19

10
4
0
1

0
7
14
4

0
26
45
18

831

832

833

834

835

836

| | C | 100 | | 10 |
|---|---|---|---|---|
| | M | 58 | | 10 |
| | Y | 0 | | 73 |
| | K | 21 | | 0 |

| | 0 | | 0 |
|---|---|---|---|
| | 9 | | 20 |
| | 50 | | 95 |
| | 24 | | 46 |

| | 0 |
|---|---|
| | 60 |
| | 100 |
| | 79 |

837

838

839

840

| C | 100 | | 0 |
|---|---|---|---|
| M | 58 | | 9 |
| Y | 0 | | 50 |
| K | 21 | | 24 |

| 0 | | 0 |
|---|---|---|
| 20 | | 3 |
| 95 | | 19 |
| 46 | | 6 |

| 10 |
|---|
| 0 |
| 33 |
| 0 |

841

842

843

844

845

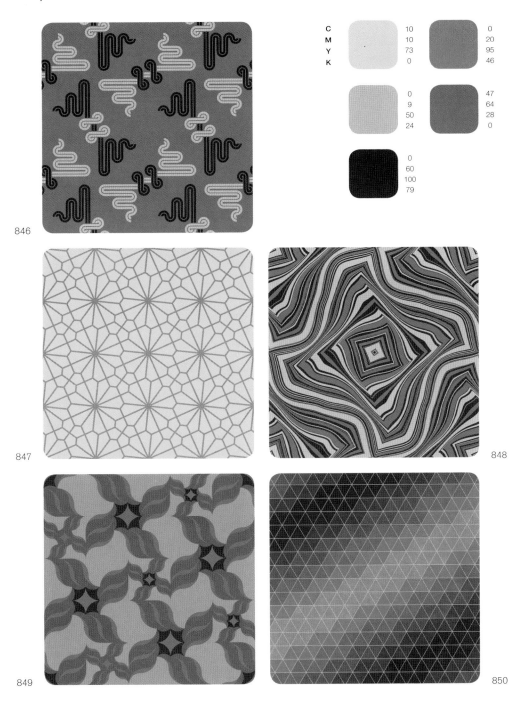

C 10    0
M 10    20
Y 73    95
K 0     46

0     47
9     64
50    28
24    0

0
60
100
79

846

847

848

849

850

| C | 10 | | 2 |
|---|----|---|---|
| M | 1 | | 0 |
| Y | 0 | | 0 |
| K | 40 | | 5 |

| | 33 | | 0 |
|---|----|---|---|
| | 4 | | 38 |
| | 0 | | 78 |
| | 72 | | 29 |

851

852

853

854

855

| | | |
|---|---|---|
| C | | 0 |
| M | | 38 |
| Y | | 78 |
| K | | 29 |

| | |
|---|---|
| 10 | |
| 1 | |
| 0 | |
| 40 | |

| | |
|---|---|
| 0 | |
| 1 | |
| 27 | |
| 6 | |

| | |
|---|---|
| 2 | |
| 0 | |
| 0 | |
| 5 | |

856

857

858

859

860

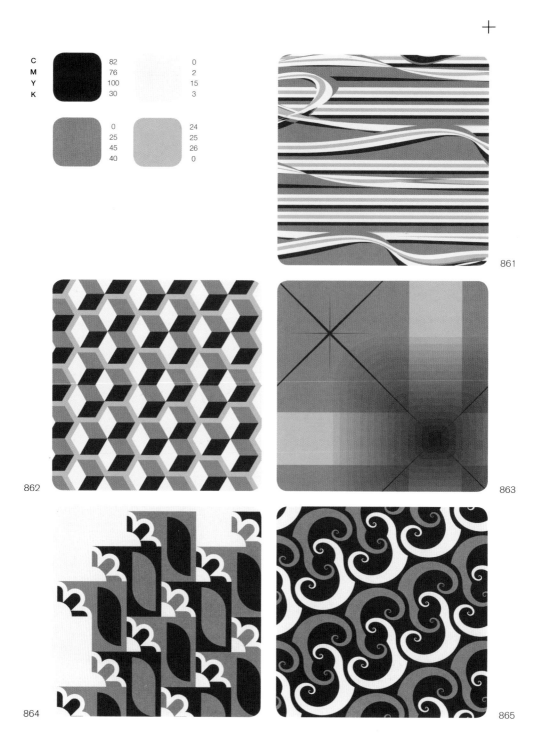

C 82 0
M 76 2
Y 100 15
K 30 3

0 24
25 25
45 26
40 0

861

862

863

864

865

866

| C | 82 | | 24 |
| M | 76 | | 25 |
| Y | 100 | | 26 |
| K | 30 | | 0 |

| | 0 | | 56 |
| | 25 | | 0 |
| | 45 | | 100 |
| | 40 | | 27 |

| | 12 |
| | 0 |
| | 29 |
| | 0 |

867

868

869

870

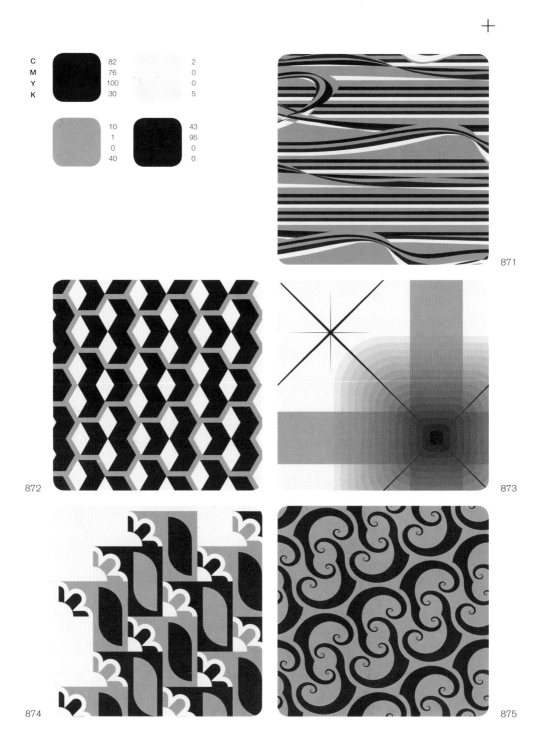

| | | |
|---|---|---|
| C | 82 | 2 |
| M | 76 | 0 |
| Y | 100 | 0 |
| K | 30 | 5 |
| | 10 | 43 |
| | 1 | 95 |
| | 0 | 0 |
| | 40 | 0 |

871

872

873

874

875

| | | |
|---|---|---|
| C | 82 | 10 |
| M | 76 | 1 |
| Y | 100 | 0 |
| K | 30 | 40 |

| | |
|---|---|
| 0 | 43 |
| 25 | 95 |
| 45 | 0 |
| 40 | 0 |

| |
|---|
| 12 |
| 0 |
| 29 |
| 0 |

876

877

878

879

880

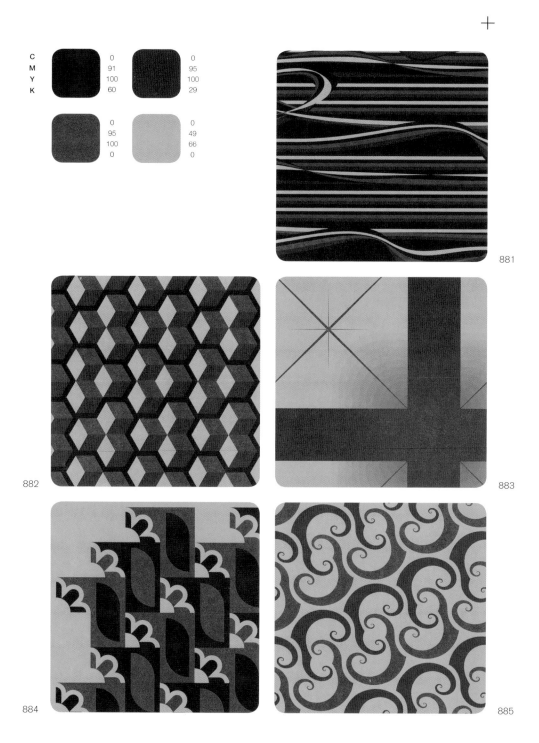

| | | | | |
|---|---|---|---|---|
| C | | 0 | | 0 |
| M | | 91 | | 95 |
| Y | | 100 | | 100 |
| K | | 60 | | 29 |
| | | 0 | | 0 |
| | | 95 | | 49 |
| | | 100 | | 66 |
| | | 0 | | 0 |

881

882

883

884

885

886

887

888

889

890

| | | |
|---|---|---|
| C | 0 | 0 |
| M | 91 | 95 |
| Y | 100 | 100 |
| K | 60 | 0 |
| | 0 | 0 |
| | 2 | 3 |
| | 87 | 10 |
| | 59 | 10 |

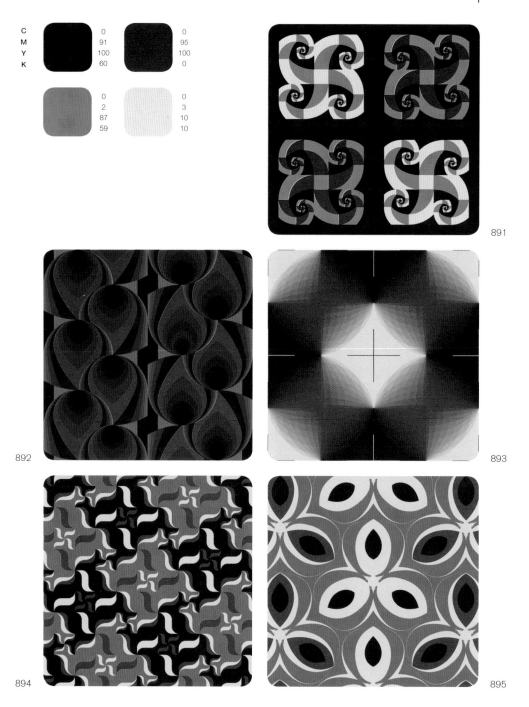

891

892

893

894

895

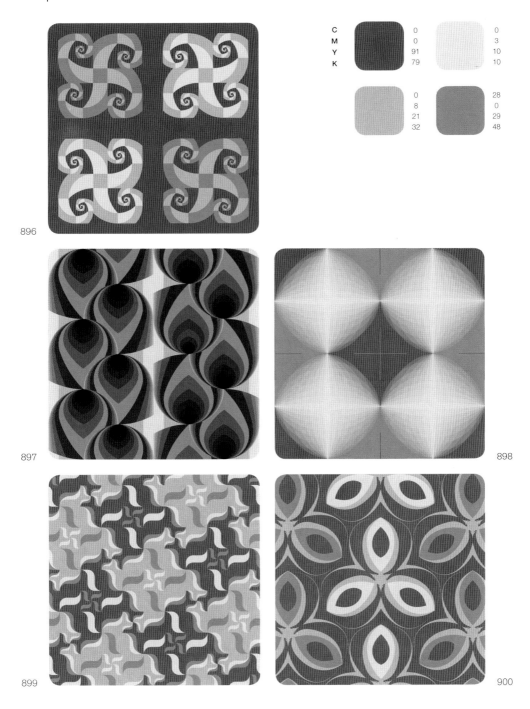

896

| | | | |
|---|---|---|---|
| C | 0 | | 0 |
| M | 0 | | 3 |
| Y | 91 | | 10 |
| K | 79 | | 10 |
| | 0 | | 28 |
| | 8 | | 0 |
| | 21 | | 29 |
| | 32 | | 48 |

897

898

899

900

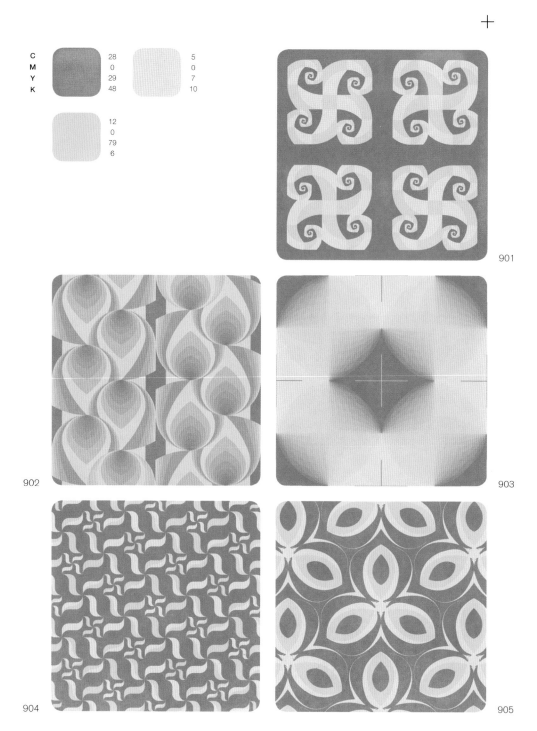

| C | 28 | | 5 |
| M | 0 | | 0 |
| Y | 29 | | 7 |
| K | 48 | | 10 |

| | 12 |
| | 0 |
| | 79 |
| | 6 |

901

902

903

904

905

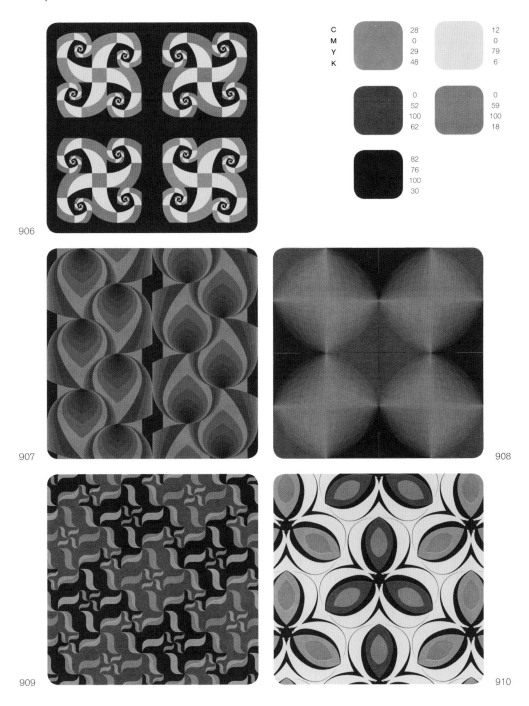

| C | 28 | | 12 |
| M | 0 | | 0 |
| Y | 29 | | 79 |
| K | 48 | | 6 |

| | 0 | | 0 |
| | 52 | | 59 |
| | 100 | | 100 |
| | 62 | | 18 |

| | 82 |
| | 76 |
| | 100 |
| | 30 |

906

907

908

909

910

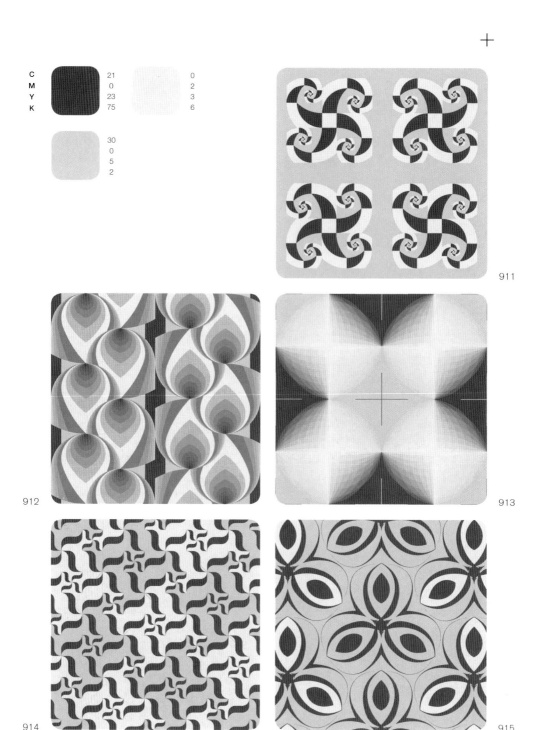

| | |
|---|---|
| C | 21 |
| M | 0 |
| Y | 23 |
| K | 75 |

| | |
|---|---|
| | 0 |
| | 2 |
| | 3 |
| | 6 |

| | |
|---|---|
| | 30 |
| | 0 |
| | 5 |
| | 2 |

911

912

913

914

915

916

| | | |
|---|---|---|
| C | 21 | 0 |
| M | 0 | 2 |
| Y | 23 | 3 |
| K | 75 | 6 |
| | 30 | 0 |
| | 0 | 11 |
| | 5 | 21 |
| | 2 | 6 |

917

918

919

920

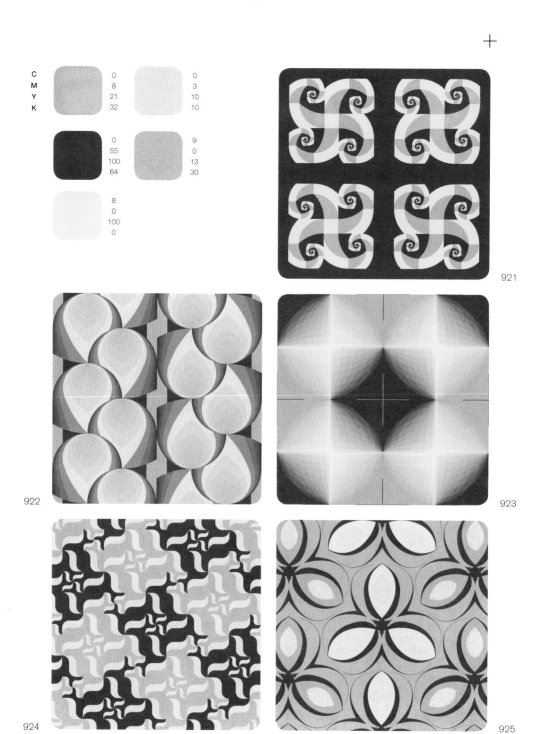

| | C | | |
|---|---|---|---|
| C | 0 | | 0 |
| M | 8 | | 3 |
| Y | 21 | | 10 |
| K | 32 | | 10 |

| | 0 | | 9 |
|---|---|---|---|
| | 55 | | 0 |
| | 100 | | 13 |
| | 64 | | 30 |

| | 8 |
|---|---|
| | 0 |
| | 100 |
| | 0 |

921

922

923

924

925

926

C 10    2
M 1    0
Y 0    0
K 40    5

33    0
4    0
0    88
72    3

927

928

929

930

C 21
M 0
Y 23
K 75

0
2
3
6

0
0
88
3

931

932

933

934

935

936

937

938

939

940

| C | 65 | | 14 |
|---|----|----|----|
| M | 55 | | 10 |
| Y | 100 | | 27 |
| K | 28 | | 0 |

| | 10 |
|---|----|
| | 10 |
| | 73 |
| | 0 |

941

942

943

944

945

946

947

948

949

950

## About the Authors

**Kathie Alexander** created all the themes and applied the color palettes to the patterns in this book. She is a freelance designer based in Peoria, Illinois. Prior to her freelance career, Alexander was employed by Dynamic Graphics/JupiterMedia for nine years, where she worked in the marketing and publishing departments. Her most recent role was art director of *Dynamic Graphics* magazine for six years.

**Harvey Rayner** created all the patterns in this book. He is a graphic and Web designer in Suffolk, England, and creator of www.root2art and www.patterncooler. com, a library database of more than 11,000 seamless patterns. Drawing on his long-held interest in programming and geometry, Rayner is now developing more powerful tools and resources to enable designers to manipulate and apply pattern design in new and inventive ways.

## About the CD-ROM

On this CD-ROM, you'll find an Adobe Illustrator (CS3) .EPS file for each of the patterns that appear in the book *Pattern and Palette Sourcebook 4*. They are organized by the image number that is printed next to each pattern in the book.

The .EPS files are scalable vector files, which can be enlarged or reduced using graphic-editing software. If there is no graphic editing software installed on your computer, you will need to download software in order to access files. All of the files are copyright-free and may be reproduced, manipulated, or reformatted for private and commercial use.

Copyright 2010 Rockport Publishers, Inc.
All rights reserved